THE ANASAZI

Prehistoric People of the Four Corners Region

by J. Richard Ambler
photography by Marc Gaede

Museum of Northern Arizona

ABOUT THE AUTHOR

Dick Ambler was born in Colorado and has lived most of his life in the Southwest. His thirty years of archaeological work has included excavations and surveys in all Four Corners states, as well as Wyoming and Texas. He holds an M.A. degree in anthropology from the University of Arizona and received his Ph.D. in anthopology from the University of Colorado in 1966. He presently is Research Professor of Anthropology Emeritus at Northern Arizona University. The Anasazi are one of his main research interests, particularly the earlier stages of their development. Currently, he is engaged in studies of the technology of the Anasazi and other prehistoric groups. He is the author of numerous technical articles and books dealing with southwestern archaeology.

ABOUT THE PHOTOGRAPHER

Marc Gaede has been a U. S. Marine Corp photographer, Curator of Photography for the Museum of Northern Arizona, temporary assistant to Ansel Adams, and Photographer in Residence at the Center for Creative Photography at the University of Arizona. Mr. Gaede holds a Bachelor of Science degree in Anthropology from Northern Arizona University and a Master of Fine Arts from Art Center College of Design.

FRONT COVER: Cliff Palace

Contents

Preface

More archaeology has been done in the southwestern United States than in any other area of comparable size in the world. After a century of excavation, archaeologists realize how little they know of the prehistoric people of the Southwest, even though the broad outlines of the story have been discernible for decades. Several major groups have been defined, among them the *Anasazi*, who lived in the region surrounding the point where the modern states of Utah, Colorado, Arizona, and New Mexico meet. Dozens of archaeologists have devoted their lifetimes to studying the Anasazi. In the process, they have written many thousands of detailed pages describing the ruins, artifacts, and lifeway of these ancient people.

This book is an attempt to reduce the voluminous technical literature to a more easily grasped visual and verbal form, condensing the information that has been so painstakingly gathered on the Anasazi. It is the efforts of several generations of archaeologists and their co-workers that have made this book possible, but in the interest of brevity and readability, references are not given in the text. For the few original ideas expressed in the following pages, I will happily take the credit or blame, but the germs for those thoughts often have been planted by others.

During the course of the preparation of this book, a number of people have been most generous with their time and talents. For making collections available for photography, allowing access to specific ruins, making helpful suggestions on the text and photographs, typing, assisting with the myriad details of publi-

cation, and general moral support, we extend our sincere thanks to the following individuals: Hermann Bleibtreu, Carolyn Cohen, K.C. and Gwen DenDooven, Deloris and Sandra Douglas, E.C. Frederick, Marsha Gallagher, Emil W. Haury, Walter and Eleanor Herriman, Ann Hitchcock, J. Earl Ingmanson, Alexander J. Lindsay, Jr., Kathryn Martin Martha Mayben, Nanci McDonald, Mark Middleton, Gertrude Muloli, Stewart L. Peckham, Dale Peterson, Norman Ritchie, Cynthia Shupert, Watson Smith, Ronald R. Switzer, Stephen Trimble, Charles B. Voll, Mr. and Mrs. E. Cardon Walker, Nancy Warren, Gilbert R. Wenger, Arthur H. White, Caroline Wilson, Mr. and Mrs. Peter G. Wray, and Richard C. Young.

During the ten years that have passed since the first edition of this brief volume was published, there has been an information explosion on the standard archaeological topics concerning the Anasazi, and new topics have begun to be explored.

My continued involvement with southwestern archaeology has heightened my interest in the Anasazi. Conversations with colleagues, students, and friends have given me moral support and helped me expand and clarify my thoughts about the Anasazi for this second edition.

Particularly helpful have been Michael S. Berry, Peter W. Bungart, Martha M. Callahan, Andrew L. Christenson, Bridget Ambler, Helen C. Fairley, Phil R. Geib, Richard H. Hevly, R. G. Matson, Linda Lay Shuler, Mary Anne Stein, and Mark Q. Sutton. Diana Lubick encouraged me to revise the text and served as editor of this second edition.

Pueblo Pintado, the most easterly of the large Chaco Canyon towns

Introduction

The first Europeans to enter what now is the Four Corners area of the Southwest, where Arizona, Utah, Colorado, and New Mexico meet, were concerned with the Indians they found living in the region, but had little interest in their ancestry and origins. The Spaniards of the sixteenth, seventeenth, and eighteenth centuries were interested primarily in converting heathens, obtaining labor for their farming and building endeavors, and fending off raids by the more nomadic groups. Although they must have seen many abandoned villages, they evidently did not think them worthy of note. Later Mexicans and Americans also displayed more concern with how they could use the native inhabitants or avoid trouble with them than with their history. Part of this lack of interest in the past occupation of the area was caused by the exigencies of frontier life, but much of it paralleled the general intellectual climate of the time.

The prehistoric ruins of the Southwest did not begin attracting attention until the last quarter of the nineteenth century—when the Navajos, Apaches, and Utes had been defeated militarily and confined to reservations, the Civil War had been concluded, and people all over the world were begining to get excited about the physical and cultural evolution of mankind. Scattered reports by news reporters, explorers, and government surveyors sparked enough interest that by the 1880s, the Smithsonian Institution and other eastern museums regularly sponsored expeditions to the Southwest in search of both prehistoric artifacts and information on the prehistoric inhabitants.

At first, these early "archaeologists" tended to concentrate their efforts south of the Four Corners region, but with the discovery of Cliff Palace and other well-preserved cliff ruins on the Mesa Verde in the late 1880s, interest shifted northward; and within a few years, most of the larger ruins in the Four Corners area had been discovered. Sites such as Mug House, Betatakin, Kiet Siel, Inscription House, Sityatki, Poncho House, Homolovi, Pueblo Bonito, Kuau-a, Tyuonyi, and many others became well known throughout archaeological circles. Many were considered too "civilized" to have been built by ancestors of modern Indians in the United States, and so we are left with names like "Aztec Ruins."

Unfortunately, it was the rule of the day to dig in a site almost as soon as it was discovered—with little concern about the location or relationships of objects. Thus, all we have to show for much of the first quarter century of unabashed digging are large collections of museum pieces. By the time of World War I, however, it was apparent to field workers that stylistic, stratigraphic, and temporal differences were present in many of the sites they were digging, and more attention was given to the location and association of objects found. At the end of the summer of 1927, southwestern archaeologists gathered at Pecos, which was being excavated by A.V. Kidder, to discuss the past summer's activities. In the course of the discussion, the archaeologists formalized the changes through time that they had been noticing in the prehistoric northern Southwest. This formalization has come to be called the "Pecos Classification." It still is used widely by archaeologists today, though with considerable refinement.

At the time of the first Pecos Conference (a similar gathering has been held almost every year since), there was the general impression that the earliest people known at that time had been replaced by later arrivals that eventually became the present day Pueblo Indians of Arizona and New Mexico. For some years, the earlier people had been termed "Basketmaker," and the later ones "Pueblo," and these terms were retained by the Pecos conferees. Since that time, it has become evident that the Basketmakers and Pueblos were part of the same cultural tradition, so a more unifying term has been thought necessary. The Navajo Indians, who apparently entered the Southwest in the 1500s, recognized that the ruins they saw were not of their ancestors and, hence, called the ancient inhabitants of the ruins "Anasazi," which, roughly translated, means "old enemies." (The Pueblos and Navajos have been on varying terms for the last four centuries, but the relationship often has been characterized by unfriendliness to downright hostility.) Most archaeologists have adopted the Navajo term, and these prehistoric people of the northern Southwest now are generally known as Anasazi.

Two years after the first Pecos conference, the historic tree-ring record was linked to the prehistoric, and, suddenly, it became possible to date old roof beams and other pieces of wood and charcoal. Tree-ring dating is so accurate that it is possible to determine the season of a particular year in which a tree was cut. At one room of Chetro Ketl in Chaco Canyon, for instance, archaeologists were able to determine that several logs were cut in the fall or winter of 1039 to 1040, another in the spring of 1040, and these were added to others that had been cut a year or two previously to roof the room in the spring or summer of 1040. Tree-ring dating is so precise and economical that southwestern archaeologists rarely use other physical dating methods such as radiocarbon dating, thermoluminescence, or obsidian hydration dating— except when the remains are older than the 2200-year-old southwestern tree-ring chronology or when suitable pieces of wood are not found.

By correlating large numbers of tree-ring dates with what else was found in the same room or site, it has become possible to define closely the time that certain architectural features became common or when specific pottery styles came into vogue, and we know now that not everyone started doing things the same way at the same time. Some Anasazi hung on to their old ways for centuries, while others eagerly were embracing new religious, social, and technical ideas. Thus, a stage of development in one part of the Anasazi area may not have been contemporaneous with another. This means that only general dates can be given for each stage. Since the Pecos classification still is widely used today as a quick reference to the level of Anasazi cultural development, we will continue its use here. A brief summary of these stages serves to set the background for more detailed discussion.

Basketmaker I: The 1927 Pecos Conference recognized that the earliest known cultural remains had to have some antecedents and postulated this stage with little specific information. We know now that 10,000 years of human occupation in the northern Southwest preceded the Anasazi development. The earliest people relied on the large Pleistocene fauna as a good supply of food and clothing. With the extinction of many forms, and increased knowledge of plants growing in various habitats, small groups of people moved frequently, often seasonally, from place to place, depending upon a more generalized gathering and hunting lifestyle for thousands of years.

Basketmaker II (abbreviated BMII): 100 B.C.(?) to A.D. 500 or 700. The Anasazi were growing corn and squash but still doing a lot of hunting and gathering. The bow and arrow had not yet been introduced, so hunting was done with spears, thrown with spear throwers, or *atlatls*. Dogs may have helped with the hunting. Basketmaker II people often lived in caves, dug pits for storing food, and, in some areas, constructed circular log houses. The term by which we call them is derived from their well-made baskets and the fact that they made no pottery.

Basketmaker III (BMIII): A.D. 500 to 700 or later. Beans were added to the food crops, and more permanent villages of several partly subterranean, circular houses became the norm. The Indians now made pottery, both plain gray and painted black-on-gray, in addition to their fine baskets. The bow and arrow partly replaced the spear and spear thrower.

Pueblo I (PI): A.D. 700 to 900. The practice of strapping babies to hard cradleboards to flatten the backs of their heads was now in vogue. The resulting deformation is the reason early archaeologists thought that a different physical type had replaced the Basketmakers. Dental studies now show us that newcomers did arrive during this period. Perhaps they found the cranial deformation attractive. Houses tended to cluster more tightly and often had adjoining walls though the earlier pit houses continued. Pottery underwent stylistic changes and became more clearly differentiated into black-on-white and plain gray. Black-on-red and red-on-orange pots also were made in some areas. The gray cooking pots showed little refinement, though the last few coils near the rim sometimes were left unsmoothed on the outside. This resulted in a neck-banded effect.

Pueblo II (PII): A.D. 900 to 1100 or 1170. The neck-banded cooking pottery became corrugated over the entire surface of the vessel. The coils were unobliterated, and finger marks show where the coils were pinched together. Black-on-white and, in some areas, black-on-red pottery continued— though generally with bolder designs. More importantly, there appears to have been a population increase during this stage. Most sites remained fairly small, with three to twenty living rooms. However, there were many more villages, some in canyons and on mesas that had not been occupied previously. At least one special room was present at almost every village, usually separated from and in front of the room block. These rooms commonly are circular and underground. Because similar rooms continue to be used in present day pueblos, those in the ancient sites are called by the Hopi term, "kiva." Anthropologists have long assumed that they were used for both religious purposes and as a sort of men's house or clan house.

Pueblo III (PIII): 1000 or 1120 to 1200 or 1300. The Anasazi during Pueblo III started grouping together into larger and larger masonry villages. Some of these villages were several stories high. Although the actual number of sites may have decreased during this stage, the population continued to increase. Population pressures, scarcity of resources, and warlike nomads (perhaps the ancestors of the modern Utes and Paiutes) led to the increasingly widespread practice of building villages in easily defensible locations, such as mesa tops and caves. Some of the marginal locations occupied by PII peoples were abandoned, but other favored areas were utilized intensively. Pottery, basketry, weaving, architecture, jewelry, and other arts reached new heights, and trade within the Anasazi area and with neighboring groups was conducted at a tremendous rate, considering all travel was by foot. However, the

Basketmaker II people stored their corn in pits dug into the sandy floors of dry caves and often lived in the same caves.

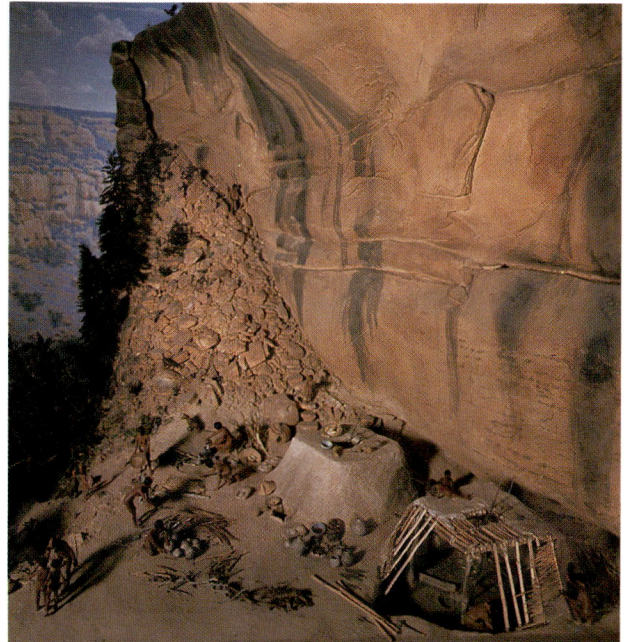

By A.D. 600, the Basketmaker III Anasazi usually lived in shallow pithouses and were making pottery in addition to baskets.

As time went on, houses became more substantial with upright adjoining walls. To feed expanding populations, the Anasazi planted large areas in corn, beans, and squash.

About A.D. 1200, many Pueblo III people moved to caves once more. Hard times and raids forced them to abandon these houses and much of their homeland, however, by the end of the century.

Anasazi had their problems with unrelated people, droughts, arroyo cutting, soil depletion, and the overuse of timber and other resources. Thus, starting in the 1100s, people began moving south, often into the sparsely populated, mountainous regions of central Arizona and New Mexico. Abandonment reached a crescendo in the late 1200s, and by 1300 the entire San Juan drainage had been abandoned.

Pueblo IV (PIV): 1300 to 1598. The northernmost Anasazi moved southward to join their relatives already living in the Hopi area, along the Little Colorado River, in the Zuni region, and near the Rio Grande. Some moved even further south and ended up in the mountains of eastern Arizona. Larger villages, housing hundreds, perhaps thousands of people, were the norm. Some archaeologists characterize this stage as "regressive," and, indeed, architecture does not show the careful construction characteristic of PIII. Some pottery (but certainly not all) was not constructed or decorated as carefully as previously, but Anasazi culture seems to have undergone a reorientation rather than a regression. Religious activities, if we are to judge by elaborate murals on the kiva walls, played an important part in peoples' lives. Yet, they did not neglect the mundane and continued a great emphasis on the arts, personal adornment, and trade. Even before the Spanish arrived, some regions, such as much of the Little Colorado River area, were abandoned. Other established villages continued to grow, and it is possible that the Anasazi would have become truly urban if the Spanish intrusion had not altered the course of events drastically. Although we often start the historic period in 1540, when Coronado entered Zuni and the Rio Grande villages, his winter stay at the village of Kuau-a in the Rio Grande had little effect. It was not until the missionaries, soldiers, and settlers arrived in 1598 that the Pueblos really felt the Spanish impact.

Pueblo V: 1598 to ? Because one of the prime Spanish goals was to abolish the Pueblo religion, they burned ceremonial masks, sacred objects, and kivas. People were whipped for not attending church, and forced labor was common. None of this endeared the Spaniards to the Pueblos. The introduction of livestock to the fragile southwestern ecology resulted in land erosion; the presence of new diseases resulted in many deaths; and the more nomadic people on all sides of the Pueblos were able to greatly increase their raiding capacity with the use of horses. Within a short time, things were a mess, and by 1680 the Pueblos had had enough. For probably the only time in their history, they acted in near unison and rebelled—killing many of the intruders and driving the remainder south to El Paso, where they stayed for twelve years, gathering courage and reinforcements. Some Pueblos fled with the Spanish, and their descendents still live near El Paso. Others, fearful of retribution, joined with the Navajo in the Gobernador region of northern New Mexico or went westward to Hopi. Many, deciding that the Spanish might be a lesser evil than the hostile tribes, returned after a few years to their Rio Grande homes. Many of these towns, however, were abandoned permanently.

There is ample reason to divide subsequent events into several stages: the Spanish influence from 1598 to 1680, the continued Spanish (and later Mexican and Anglo) influence from 1692 to the 1880s, and the reservation period (accompanied by formal schooling since the 1880s).

It is easy to argue that since 1960 or 1970 a new era has started—TV in most pueblos, the Indian art boom, the universal use of pickup trucks and cars, a newly awakened pride in being Indian, industry, tourism, land claim settlements, more schooling, and more self-determination. All have played a part in shaping Pueblo culture today. Under the fierce acculturation pressures, the Pueblos have changed but not lost many of their old customs, crafts, and beliefs. We can no more predict the course of Indian culture in the next 100 years than we can for any other group in the world, but in view of the tenacity of their culture in the face of past events, it seems likely that the Pueblos have a future as long as their past.

The prehistoric Anasazi did not live in a cultural vacuum. Surrounding them on every side were other prehistoric groups who both influenced and were influenced by the Anasazi. To the archaeologically little-known north, in central Colorado, lived scattered groups of hunters and gatherers, probably ancestors of the Utes. The Great Plains to the immediate east of the Rocky Mountains were sparsely occupied, mostly by bison hunters, but the Anasazi made periodic forays into the area, established some settlements, and did some bison hunting. To the northwest, over most of Utah, Anasazi ideas—including corn agriculture and pottery—were adopted for a few hundred years. These peoples, whom archaeologists call Fremont, never fully participated in the Anasazi cultural pattern and by about A.D. 1200 disappear from the archaeological record. Some may have joined their friends, the Anasazi, to the south; others may have gone back to hunting and gathering. The fate of the Fremont is unknown.

The modern Pueblo Indians, like those seen here at Taos, live in towns closely resembling those of their Anasazi ancestors.

Some archaeologists believed that they became Paiutes, but it now appears that the Paiute and Ute came out of eastern California, reaching the Southwest in the 1200s. To the southwest, from the San Francisco Peaks to the Grand Canyon, in the area historically claimed by the Havasupai, lived a group of people known to archaeologists as Cohonina. The Cohonina, like the Anasazi, were farmers and pottery makers. Apparently, however, they relied more on hunting than their neighbors to the northeast and never lived in large settlements.

The area to the southeast of the San Francisco Peaks was the domain of a prehistoric group called Sinagua, who were in direct contact with the most southwesterly Anasazi groups. The traditional Sinagua home was a deep pit house, but by 1100 they, too, started building masonry surface houses and (by 1200 to 1300) large pueblos. The Sinagua made a plain, brownware pottery, but they liked to trade with the Anasazi for painted pots.

The eruption of Sunset Crater in 1065 was a major event for the Sinagua. The volcano continued erupting for several years, creating a moisture-retaining mulch of fine cinders. When things calmed down, those who stuck it out found that it was easier to grow crops in the cindered areas. Coincidentally, the latter part of the eleventh century saw exceptionally good moisture. These conditions encouraged newcomers from different regions to move into the Flagstaff area. As their population grew, the Sinagua adopted a number of Anasazi ideas and became important socially, economically, and ceremonially in the Southwest. Some Anasazi moved to the Wupatki area in the 1100s. They may have joined with the Sinagua in their general movement eastward during the thirteenth century to the Winslow area—and perhaps from there, a century later, to Hopi.

South of the Anasazi, stretching across central Arizona and New Mexico, were the Mogollon. The Mogollon tradition is not well understood, perhaps because of the variation from one area to another. It is characterized by the use of brown pottery and pit houses clustered in small villages. It appears that early in Anasazi history the Mogollon were a source of some basic southern ideas, such as corn agriculture and pottery making. But by A.D. 1000, the situation had reversed, and Anasazi influence on the Mogollon was quite pronounced. Indeed, many Anasazi actually moved to the Mogollon area, introducing new architectural techniques, new pottery styles, and new religious ideas to the Mogollon. By the 1300s, the Mogollon were living in large, masonry pueblos like the Anasazi, and their culture had changed so much that it might even be called Anasazi. All these towns were abandoned and the area *despoblado* by the time Coronado came through on his search for the seven golden cities.

5

Southwest of the Mogollon, in the Arizona desert, lived the Hohokam, who, in many ways, were the most sophisticated and urban of the prehistoric southwesterners. The Hohokam appear to have migrated out of northern Mexico about 300 B.C. and to have retained many ties with the civilizations to the south. Trade from the south included shell jewelry, copper bells, macaws (parrots), and other paraphernalia, some of which found it way to the Anasazi. In exchange, the Anasazi probably traded turquoise, which was prized all the way to southern Mexico.

To support agriculture in the desert, the Hohokam built a huge system of irrigation canals much like that of their Mesoamerican neighbors to the south. The Anasazi knew a good thing when they saw it and started irrigating in the tenth or eleventh century. They never gave up their kivas, however, for ball courts. Faced with droughts, flash floods, caliche ruining the soil, and a breakdown of contact with Mesoamerica because of the collapse of the Tula empire that preceded the Aztecs, the Hohokam gave up their extensive farms and turned to individual gardening, hunting, and gathering in the 1400s. With such a complete change of lifeway, it is difficult to trace their descendents, but they appear to be the modern Pima.

Ultimately, the Anasazi owe much of their culture to Mesoamerica. It was in what now is Mexico that corn, beans, and squash first were domesticated (along with a host of other de-lectables that the Anasazi never grew, such as chilis, avocados, tomatoes, and pineapples). Pottery was made there earlier than anywhere else in North America, and religious ideas seem to have sprung up in Mesoamerica and spread out like mushrooms. By the time most of the Mesoamerican ideas reached the Anasazi, they had passed through so many hands and minds that they hardly are recognizable as Mesoamerican, and it is mainly by the trade goods and general resemblances that we can see the southern influence on the Anasazi.

Although it is clear that the Anasazi were both receivers and donors of ideas with all of their neighbors, they retained their own identity because they shared a lifeway that differed from that of their neighbors. On the other hand, even today—with our fast transportation and communication networks—there are cultural differences across northern Arizona and New Mexico. We know that the Anasazi also were not all alike. Regional difference among the Anasazi is observable, particularly by Pueblo II. In southwestern Colorado, and extending into southeastern Utah, were the Mesa Verde group ("Branch" to many archaeologists) of Anasazi, who, during PIII, made fine masonry structures with the rocks carefully pecked to the proper shape. They also made attractive black-on-white pottery. West and south of Mesa Verde is the Kayenta area. The Kayenta people never excelled in architectural activities but made excellent pottery—including black-on-

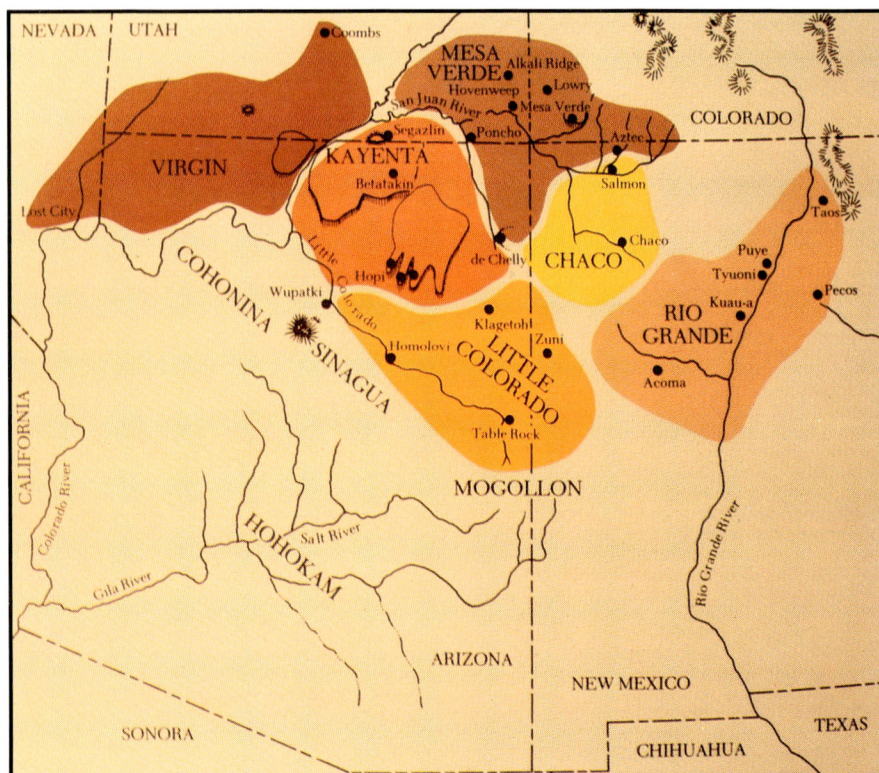

The Anasazi lived over a broad area of the Four Corners country, bounded on all sides by other prehistoric groups. A great deal of trade and interchange of ideas occurred between different Anasazi groups and between the Anasazi and their neighbors.

white, black-on-red, and polychrome—that was traded widely.

During the 1000s and 1100s, the peak of Anasazi culture may have been reached in Chaco Canyon. Architecture literally reached great heights—with pueblos containing up to 800 rooms and rising at least four stories. The walls obviously were massive in such structures, yet they were faced carefully with stones of different sizes. Much of Chaco life seems to have centered around religion, for both kivas and great kivas abound. Communication with neighboring areas also was important, and Chaco commerce and social life was enhanced by the construction of well-made roads radiating out in many directions.

East of Chaco, many Anasazi lived along the Rio Grande. These people seemed to have had close ties with those in the Mesa Verde area. When the Anasazi left Mesa Verde, there are clear indications that they joined their friends in the Rio Grande area.

South of the Kayenta Anasazi were others living in the drainage of the Little Colorado River. Partly because of the paucity of archaeological work in this area and partly because of the complexity of the prehistoric picture (which includes strong influences from the Mogollon), this group may be the least understood of the Anasazi.

West of the Kayenta area proper, in what is known today as the "Arizona Strip," lived a group variously termed "Western Kayenta" or "Virgin Branch" (named for the Virgin River). These people were similar to the Kayenta but may have lived in their large villages during the winter, scattering to family farmsteads for the summer. This area was abandoned by the Anasazi about 1150, probably because of Paiute incursions. The Virgin folks apparently joined their friends, the Kayenta. Some sites without kivas, such as Betatakin, may have been founded by these refugees from the west.

The boundaries between these major groups of Anasazi were diffuse, with a lot of overlap, and they shifted through time. In addition, not all Kayentas, or Mesa Verdeans, etc., were the same; there was almost as much variation within one of these groupings as between them. It is not surprising to find regional differences among the prehistoric Anasazi, for we have plenty of evidence for variation among their descendents, the modern Pueblo Indians. Modern variation includes differences in religion, in basic social organization, and in language. Linguistic differences range from dialect variations to completely different languages that are not even remotely related. Archaeologically, of course, it is difficult to recognize linguistic, social, and ceremonial differences.

In the past two decades, however, a lot of archaeological emphasis has been placed on determining socio-cultural patterns from the physical remains recovered by archaeologists. New techniques, such as trace element analysis, are being used to detect differences in ceramics. It is possible to see substantial variation in the Anasazi cultural pattern, and archaeologists hope that the differences they recognize are similar to those recognized by the people themselves many centuries ago.

When archaeology is performed with care, it is possible to define subtle differences within the culture; many of these differences have been dignified by names. Thus, we have several hundred regional and temporal prehistoric variations called by specific terms, such as "Klethla Focus," "Piedra Phase," and "Wepo Phase," which will not be used here. However, it should be remembered that when we are talking about the Anasazi, or Pueblo II, or the Chaco area, we are dealing in generalities. Each Anasazi village was tied to others culturally, linguistically, socially, and economically; but it appears likely that each was largely independent, and the people of each village may have prided themselves on their individuality.

One of the goals of late twentieth century archaeology is to define cultural boundaries. It now appears that the Anasazi had no formal social groups larger than the village and that a village resembled its neighbor in any combination of architecture or crafts. Transition zones, rather than boundaries, seem to have been the case.

Archaeologists, at least in their formal reports, often seem to forget that the objects and structures they are studying were made by people. In the case of the Anasazi, these people were slightly shorter than the average today, had straight black hair, and spoke in tongues unintelligible to the Western ear. They were people worried about their crops and children—remembering the past and wondering about the future. Perhaps the main difference between the Anasazi and people today is that it is unlikely that any Anasazi noticed much cultural change in the course of a lifetime. Even the briefest phases archaeologists have defined usually are over fifty years, and few Anasazi lived longer than that. With some exceptions, such as natural disasters, life would have seemed much the same from year to year for the Anasazi. One hopes that this led to a calmer and saner life with more inner peace than often is evident today, but this borders on romanticizing, and there is no evidence for it.

Basketmaker II dart foreshafts with points from Sand Dune Cave. When used, these foreshafts were slipped into the socketed front end of the spears.

Making a Living

Every Anasazi woman spent long hours grinding corn. (Top) Basketmaker II grinding slab and one-hand mano; (bottom) Pueblo II slab metate and two-hand mano

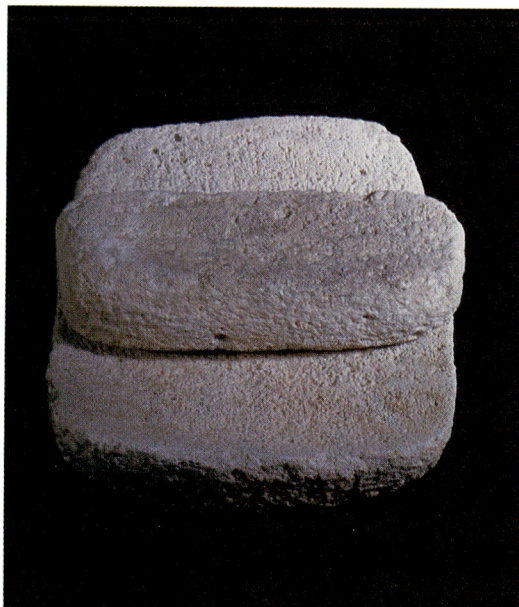

The basis of Anasazi life was agriculture, and the basic crop was maize, or what we in the United States usually call corn. The first corn in the Southwest was hardly bigger than a large grass in either stem or cob size, but after many years of selection, and the introduction of better varieties from the south by the time of Basketmaker II, the cobs were almost a large as many seen in today's supermarkets.

Although corn often was eaten fresh off the cob, one of its great advantages is that it can be stored dry for many months—and even years. BMII people ground this dried corn on pieces of stone, either shallow basin or trough metates, with a smaller stone, or mano. This corn flour apparently was then made into flat breads or cakes. With the later introduction of pottery, mush, stews, and hominy became easier to prepare and store and, thus, more common.

BMII people also grew squash very much like modern pumpkins (the same species, as a matter of fact) but possibly more for the seeds than the flesh, though it is possible to dry pumpkin flesh. It is doubtful that more than a third of the BMII diet came from corn and squash.

Hunting of deer, mountain sheep, rabbits, birds, and smaller animals probably occupied a great deal of the men's time and energy. Also, the women gathered wild seeds to supplement the diet. These seeds were important, for they, too, could be stored for the long winter months. Even the tiny ones were collected carefully, and larger ones, such as pinyon nuts, certainly were not ignored.

Seed gathering was something the people knew well because their ancestors had been doing it for thousands of years. Over time, they developed some special equipment for this activity. Seed beaters, made of a bunch of stocks tied together, are found in many Basketmaker II sites,

Some chipped stone knives, such as these Pueblo II examples, were hafted. These knives may have been ceremonial in function.

Many chipped stone knives and scrapers were simply held in the hand to use.

Arrows and other straight sticks were shaped with the aid of grooved shaft-smoothers used in pairs.

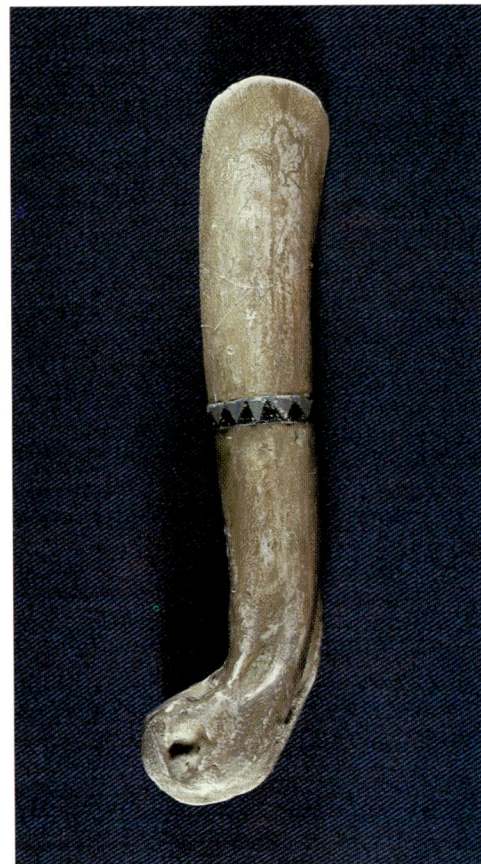

This carefully shaped and inlaid bone tool from Chaco Canyon may have been used for scraping flesh from hides.

along with large carrying baskets. Most of these BMII large baskets were conical, with a large opening, so that a woman carrying one on her back could simply throw things over her shoulder into the basket. Seeds, including corn, often were parched by putting them in a large, flat basket with hot coals. The basket had to be shaken frequently so that the seeds cooked without burning the basket, but we have found many fragments of baskets charred on the inside, indicating that eventually the basket disintegrated.

During the BMIII stage, the Anasazi started to grow beans, a significant improvement to the diet because of the added protein. Beans and corn are particularly good together because corn protein lacks an essential amino acid, lysine, which beans have in abundance, thus making the combination a more well-rounded food source. Even beans and corn together are not a complete source of all the proteins necessary for humans, however, especially for nursing mothers and young children. When hunting was poor, malnutrition could result, and the bones of some Anasazi children show this.

Since it is difficult to parch dry beans or to grind them into flour, it is no coincidence that pottery appeared among the Anasazi at the same time as beans, during BMIII. With the increased dependence upon agriculture from BMIII on, the Anasazi looked for more and more ways to increase the crop.

The introduction of a new variety of eight-rowed corn around A.D. 1000 helped, for it was more drought resistant, could be grown in a wider range of environments, and was easier to grind. About the same time, the Anasazi became concerned with getting as much water to the crops as possible, and irrigation ditches, check dams, new methods of floodwater farming, and other water control systems became common.

A third variable, wind, also was important. Blowing sand can destroy young corn plants, so the Anasazi probably protected them by constructing brush shelters for the field, as modern Hopis farming in sand often do. Since Hopi farmers also use large tin cans to protect clumps of young corn plants, it is possible that the Anasazi may have used large potsherds for the same purpose.

The eleventh century was a time of increased moisture and generally favorable climatic conditions. With the good climate, new corn, and irrigation techniques, the Pueblo II Anasazi increased greatly in numbers. Villages became established in places that hitherto never had been occupied permanently; towns grew larger, and a Pueblo II

lifeway spread far beyond the Anasazi borders. By 1150, however, the climatic cycle was reversing itself again; the Southwest was getting drier, and it would not be until 1700 that optimum conditions would again prevail.

The Anasazi had weathered a previous dry cycle and numerous short-term droughts, but now things were different. Populations were at an all-time high, large areas had been deforested for building materials and firewood, and the sandy soils had lost most of their nutrients because of intensive cultivation.

As the dryness increased, crops became poorer, and arroyo cutting began. Entire areas were abandoned, with the survivors moving in search of suitable cropland and other resources. The poor climatic conditions were exacerbated by the fact that Utes were moving in from the north and Paiutes from the west. The Virgin Kayenta, yielding to Paiute pressure, joined their friends and relatives in the Kayenta area during the latter half of the 1100s. Chaco Canyon was completely deserted by 1150, probably because of arroyo cutting.

There was a brief reoccupation of the Chaco almost a century later by people of Mesa Verde affiliation. All the rest of the San Juan was abandoned by 1300.

In the face of adverse circumstances, the Anasazi had to practice even more intensive farming. By this time, however, they had developed varieties of corn that could be planted a foot or more deep in the sand to take advantage of subsurface moisture. The Anasazi weathered the dry spell, but their lives had changed substantially.

The only domestic animals kept by the Anasazi were turkeys and dogs. Turkeys appear to have been kept more for their feathers than for their meat. Dogs probably were useful as guards and as a source of soft fur—though they may have been eaten when food was scarce.

One practice that helped the Anasazi through hard times was a continued dependence on hunting and gathering. The bow and arrow replaced the spear and spear-thrower during BMIII, and various nets, snares, and traps also were in common use.

As a rough estimate, hunting and gathering continued to supply perhaps half of the total dietary intake. The growing of a good crop often was the determining factor on how well a group made it through the winter, but drought also affects wild foods. Anasazi life, therefore, was closely bound to land and water, and a good deal of physical and religious energy was expended to assure an adequate supply of both.

The back portion of Cave du Pont was almost filled by Basketmaker II slab-lined storage cists, shown here many years after the archaeological excavation.

Making a Home

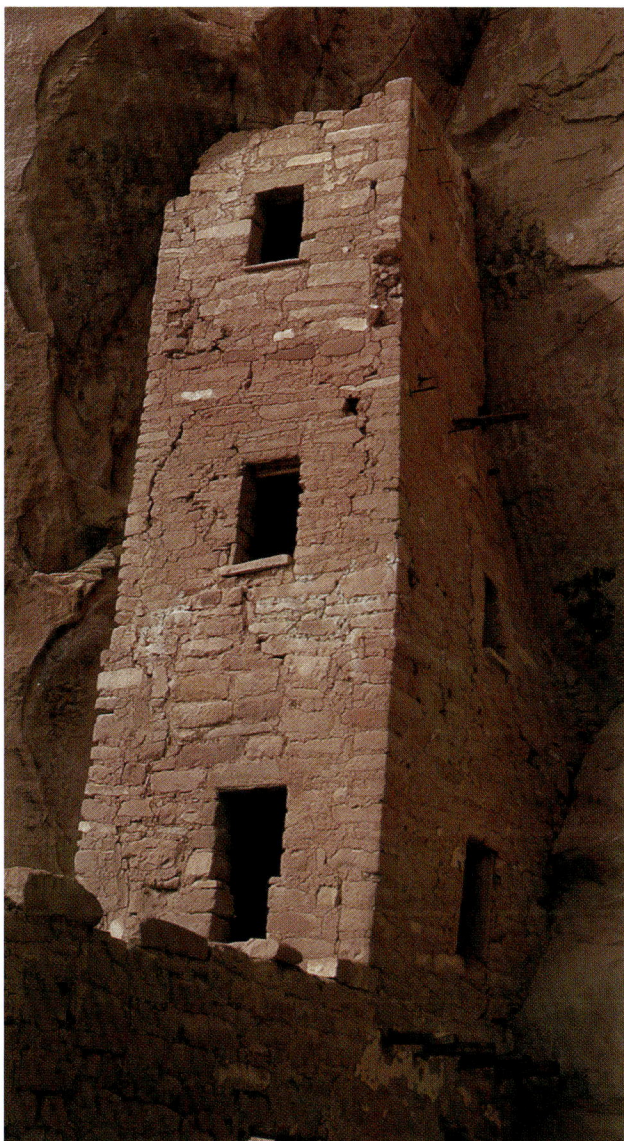

Square Tower House, Mesa Verde

Perhaps the Basketmaker I people constructed some shelters, but it seems that the early hunters and gatherers of the Southwest moved frequently and thus spent little time on house building. Since the BMII people had crops to plant, tend, and harvest, they probably lived near their fields at least part of the growing season. With a good supply of corn and other seeds to store for the winter, they may have been able to spend the coldest months in semi-permanent residences. However, we have good evidence for BMII houses only in the upper eastern portions of the San Juan drainage. The BMII houses in what now is southwestern Colorado were circular, mostly 10 to 25 feet in diameter. The loose surface sand was scraped away to make a saucer-shaped floor with a fire ring in the center. The walls were made of logs, cribbed inward toward the smokehole in the roof. The wall surface probably was covered with mud, so that the total would have been very much like Navajo cribbed log hogans still seen in the Four Corners country today. Basketmaker II people, like the Navajo, lived in families or small groups of families that were spread widely over the landscape. Farther east, in the Los Piños River area, these houses usually had large, circular "antechambers" or entry rooms to one side and often had cobble pavements around all or part of the outside.

To the west of the Four Corners, BMII houses have been found only rarely and have been excavated even more rarely. Much of the landscape yields no sites at all. Apparently, BMII people in this area did not bother with houses. They lived in the open during good weather and in caves when it was too hot, too cold, too windy, or too wet.

Caves were valuable to the BMII people because here they could store their grain without worrying about the damp; be protected from the rain, snow, and wind; and keep warm from a protected fire. With the dry southwestern climate, corn can be stored easily in these caves, and some still is preserved after almost 2000 years. The

Indians usually stored corn and other items in pits dug into the ground, which then were covered with logs or small mud domes. Where the ground was sandy, as in most caves, the pits were lined with upright sandstone slabs and chinked with juniper bark and mud to keep out both sand and rodents. Occasionally, these storage cists were large enough that it would have been possible, though crowded, to live in them—or at least sleep in them. Some caves were used for both living and storage, but others served almost entirely for storage or burial, often with burials made in the older storage cists.

By Basketmaker III times, more families were grouping together, often living in villages of from ten to twenty households. Houses from different times and places vary, and even those at a single village were not all the same. Most BMIII people chose to live in a large, circular house with a floor one to three feet below the surface. Pit houses were warm in the winter and cool in the summer. Many houses had circular entryways on the southeastern side of the house; this orientation to the southeast continued through PIII—partly because of the prevailing wind pattern, which is from the southwest. Strong winds, however, often come from the west or north. Having the house doorway facing the southeast was also a help in letting the morning sun into the house during the cold days of winter.

The roof usually was supported by four posts and had a smokehole aligned with the central firepit below. Many BMII pit houses had wing walls extending from the firepit to the walls on either side of the entry. These wing walls, from a few inches to several feet high, obviously served to partition the room—with the major household activities taking place in the larger portion of the house.

Often, a slab for grinding corn and other seeds stood adjacent to the wing wall, inside the main portion of the house. Archaeologists often find an upright slab or similar contrivance between the firepit and the entry, or even next to the firepit, which seems to have served largely to break up the entering air current. This upright slab is referred to as a deflector. Often, the wing walls themselves served to dissipate cold air, but their main function may have been to keep crawling babies and toddlers inside the main part of the house, or to keep dogs from entering. In the main part of the house, halfway between the firepit and the rear wall, a small hole often is found. Judging by analogy with modern Pueblo beliefs, this hole served as a representation of the Sipapu, the mythical hole where their ancestors emerged into this world from the one below.

Pueblo II ruin, Chaco Canyon. Often, women would get together in one room to grind the day's corn and talk.

T-shaped doorways may have had a special religious significance. This one at Pueblo Bonito is tall enough that many of the ruin's inhabitants could have walked through without stooping.

Storage pits are found within some BMIII houses, but the storing of grain more typically was done in small bins behind the houses. By Pueblo I times, these bins were getting larger, and many of them were serving as housing, at least during the summer. In some areas, especially by the end of Pueblo I, practically everyone in villages was living in these surface rooms. Pit houses out in front were used for religious observances and, perhaps, as winter habitations. A few such proto-kivas have been found in BMIII sites, such as Shabikeshchee Village in Chaco Canyon. The presence of two very large cists, in front of the smaller ones at the BMII site of Cave du Pont, suggests that the idea of a distinct structure in front of the others started well before we can call them kivas. Ceremonial activities became more important as time passed, though it was not until Pueblo IV that we are confident that the distinct structures served almost entirely as religious structures and can truly be called kivas. In Pueblo II and III, these structures served many functions other than religion, but the term "kiva" is used widely and will be retained.

The practice of building rooms next to each other necessitated an upright, rather than a sloping, wall, so new construction techniques came into use. A frequently used method was to ram posts into the ground and fill the spaces between the posts with smaller sticks, stones, or clay—or any combination of these. This jacal or wattle-and-daub type of construction continued to be used by the Anasazi for centuries, though it was replaced gradually by sturdier construction.

By Pueblo II times, many people were building masonry houses, with walls of stones and mud mortar and roofs of horizontal beams covered with smaller sticks, juniper bark, and, finally, mud. Frequently, a village was composed of a row or two of contiguous living and storage rooms—with their doors opening generally in an easterly, southeasterly, or southerly direction so the warming effect of the winter sun would be felt. A short distance away, either in the same direction or incorporated into the room block, would be one or more kivas. Many Pueblo II sites were small, housing only a few families, but some had scores of rooms. PII people in the Kayenta area appear to have been more conservative, at least architecturally, since many continued to live in pit houses.

One of the hallmarks of Pueblo III was the construction of large, masonry pueblos. The largest of these, Pueblo Bonito in Chaco Canyon, began with about twenty rooms in A.D. 1000. By 1150, it had reached over 800 rooms and kivas and rose at least four stories high. To be made that

Masonry styles changed through time. Early Chaco masonry (upper left) was somewhat cruder than the later banded styles.

Jacal construction was common during Pueblo I, II, and III. This partly restored example is at Inscription House west of Betatakin (right).

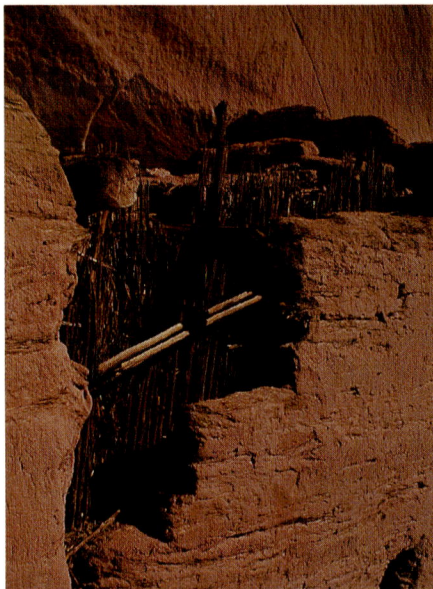

Many of the ceilings at Pueblo Bonito have disintegrated with the passage of time, but the sturdily constructed walls often remain intact.

Long House back wall shows careful attention to detailed fitting.

Pueblo Alto in Chaco Canyon

high, Chaco masonry had to be massive and thick. Yet, because of the banded surfaces, it has a certain grace and delicacy. Wall exteriors were finished by carefully alternating layers of thin and thick slabs in several different styles. The inside mass of the wall was filled with miscellaneous rocks, rubble, sand, and clay. By PIII times, there were distinct differences in village size—with perhaps one very large site containing many kivas, several smaller, permanently occupied sites with two or three kivas, and numerous one-kiva sites in a typical ten-square- mile area. Some larger sites in the Mesa Verde area often are thought of as Chaco outliers because of the construction techniques used there. It is clear, however, that their trade relationships, at least in pottery, were better established with the Kayenta, while their kiva styles are more like those of Mesa Verde than Chaco.

Mesa Verde walls typically were made by carefully pecking each sandstone block to a standard size and setting these blocks into mud mortar. The Kayentans continued to be unconcerned with wall-finishing styles developed elsewhere and typically constructed walls of unshaped rocks, filling in the irregularities (especially on the inside of a room) with smaller ones. Some Kayentans remained in pit houses through Pueblo III. A

Balcony House. Pueblo III kivas had masonry linings. They were roofed by resting logs on the upright pilasters and then cribbing them in toward the center, leaving a hole in the center for an entryway and smokehole.

few of these pit houses were built in places where building stone was scarce, but others were constructed alongside masonry rooms. Although some of these pit houses were used for special purposes, such as weaving or grinding corn, most served as living rooms. Many surface living rooms had the front (or southeast) wall made of jacal.

Rooms generally were small, with small doors, though Chaco rooms and doorways are larger than those in the Mesa Verde or Kayenta areas. The doors could be closed easily with a mat or a

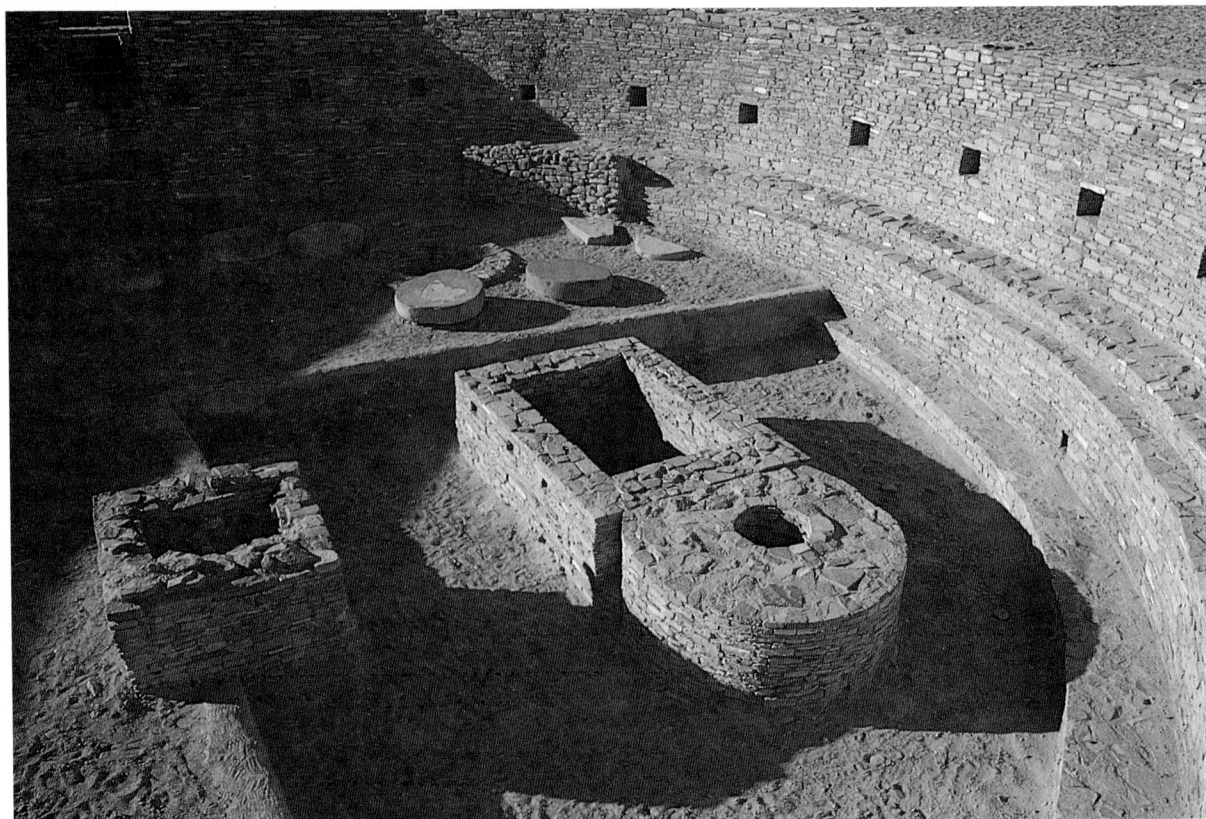

Some communities in the Chaco and Mesa Verde areas had great kivas. In this great kiva at Chetro Ketl, four circular masonry units enclosed the huge roof supports. The adjacent rectangular box, which may have been covered by plants, served as a foot drum.

18

Inscription House. Pueblo rooms were roofed with large beams covered by smaller sticks, bark, and clay (top). Some kivas in protected caves still have their roofs and show the intense soot blackening that resulted from the central fire (bottom).

hide to keep out drafts, and storage rooms usually were sealed with a tight-fitting stone slab—secured by sticks to make them rodent-proof. Storage rooms often had hard-packed or slab-paved floors and a few pegs in the walls for hanging things. Otherwise, they were bare. Living rooms usually had central firepits, and those in the Kayenta area often were connected to the wall on either side of the doorway by upright slabs, mak-

ing an entrybox reminiscent of the BMIII wing walls.

Many rooms contained a mealing bin, but in pueblos with more internal unity, mealing bins often were grouped together. This allowed several women to get together and chat while grinding the day's cornmeal. Metates often were arranged in a series to grind from coarse to fine. Mealing rooms seem to have been more common during PII than

Pueblo Alto West may have served as an entry point for Chaco Canyon since several prehistoric roads converge in this locale on the north rim of the canyon.

PIII, which may be a reflection of increasing village strife during PIII, despite (or because of) the larger village size.

Other household furnishings generally were sparse. From houses that burned suddenly, we can see that most houses from BMIII times on generally contained a variety of cooking, eating, and storage pots; some baskets and clothing; and other equipment, such as bows and arrows, digging sticks, hammerstones, mauls and axes, bone awls, drills, scrapers, and knives. Living, eating, and sleeping were done on the floor, with no furniture as we know it today.

General similarities are found among most of the Anasazi kivas, but each region had its own distinctive features. Kivas usually were circular in plan and as completely subterranean as possible—even if this meant carving the floor into bedrock or building up retaining walls around the kiva to make it appear underground. Most kivas had an encircling shelf or "bench" several feet above the floor. Upon this were masonry columns, or pilasters, that supported the cribbed log roof. In the

Stone axes were ground carefully out of hard rocks, then hafted with somewhat flexible handles.

20

Kayenta and Mesa Verde areas, and to a lesser degree in Chaco, many kivas had an alcove or recess on the southeasterly side, at the same level as the bench. This southern recess, probably a carryover from the old antechamber, gives many kivas a keyhole-shaped appearance.

Kivas had central firepits, and the roof entryway also served as a smokehole. Fresh air was provided by a ventilator shaft from the ground level outside, connected to a tunnel entering under the southern recess at or below floor level. Between the ventilator and firepit was a deflector made of masonry, slab, or jacal. A sipapu, representing the place of emergence from the previous world and the communication link to the spirit world, frequently is found between the firepit and back wall. Occasionally, a circular slab or other special feature appears in place of this hole. Ashpits often are found adjacent to the firepit, and foot-drums, niches, and other features also occur. Loom holes to anchor the bottom of an upright loom are common.

The presence of looms in kivas is no surprise, for Pueblo men to this day often weave in the kivas. Since weaving is a winter activity, it seems likely that it would be carried out in winter habitations. Kivas have been used more by men than women in historic times, and this pattern probably became established by Pueblo IV.

The kiva thus served not only as a religious center, but also as a sort of clubhouse as well. This helps to ease tensions in the modern Pueblo societies that are matrilocal (where all the women in a village are closely related and men are treated almost as outsiders). Prehistoric men may have felt the same need for a place they could call their own. The large number of kivas at some PIII sites at Yellowjacket, west of Mesa Verde, raises questions about habitation units, ceremonial life, and social relationships.

The Chaco and, to a lesser extent, Mesa Verde Anasazi also built great kivas—circular structures fifty or more feet in diameter, with huge pillars or posts supporting the roof, raised firepits, foot-drums, and occasionally elaborate entries. The great kivas were not simply larger versions of the small ones, nor did they appear suddenly. They occurred as early as BMIII (though they were not very elaborate this early) and are found even earlier among the Mogollon to the south. It appears that the small kivas were associated with certain families but that the activities in the great kivas were the concern of large groups of people. These structures, where women as well as men may have had key roles, can properly be called kivas.

During the thirteenth century, the Anasazi started choosing more easily defended locations for their villages. Depending on the local terrain,

Pueblo Bonito in Chaco Canyon was one of the largest Anasazi communities. Perhaps as many as a thousand people lived here nine centuries ago.

Hovenweep. In parts of the Mesa Verde area, Pueblo III people built towers near the heads of canyons—perhaps to guard the precious springs.

Chetro Ketl is an excellent example of Pueblo masonry skills.

The builders of Betatakin found it necessary to compensate for the steeply sloping cave floor by carving out spaces for wall foundations and piling dirt and trash behind retaining walls.

this meant that dwellings were constructed on the tops of steep-sided little mesas, nearly inaccessible caves, promontories, and other places difficult to reach. Where necessary, the Anasazi protected these sites even more by building defensive walls. There is no question that many of these late PIII sites are defensive in nature. Intervillage strife is a possibility, but since the Anasazi continued a lively trade with each other, fighting with the neighbors is unlikely. The outsiders that arrived in the Four Corners area during this period are the Utes and their relatives, the Paiutes. These groups had a practice of making devastating raids to drive the local inhabitants away from their home so they could live on their stored supplies until they ran out. They then repeated this pattern with the next village. They were successful, finally, in driving the Anasazi from the Four Corners area. It is no coincidence that Anasazi settlements on the west (where the Paiutes were) and north (the direction from which the Utes came) were the first to be abandoned.

With the abandonment of the San Juan drain-age by the end of PIII (about A.D. 1300), and a general movement southward, towns continued to grow in size, but construction was cruder. Pueblo IV rooms often were larger than those built during PIII—though as sparsely furnished. Kivas in Hopi regions to the west commonly were rectangular; in the Zuni area, they were circular, and in the Rio Grande, they were a variety of sizes and shapes. With a few possible exceptions, great kivas were no longer made. Sometimes, the PIV larger villages were built as one cohesive mass of rooms; more frequently, they were divided physically into several neighboring room blocks separated by plazas or streets.

The coming of the Spanish settlers, soldiers, and missionaries put an abrupt halt to what may have developed into another Anasazi cultural peak with even larger towns. Although many modern Pueblos still retain the flavor of the prehistoric towns and more complex architecture. European influence is seen today in the presence of larger doorways, glassed windows, bread ovens, and mission churches.

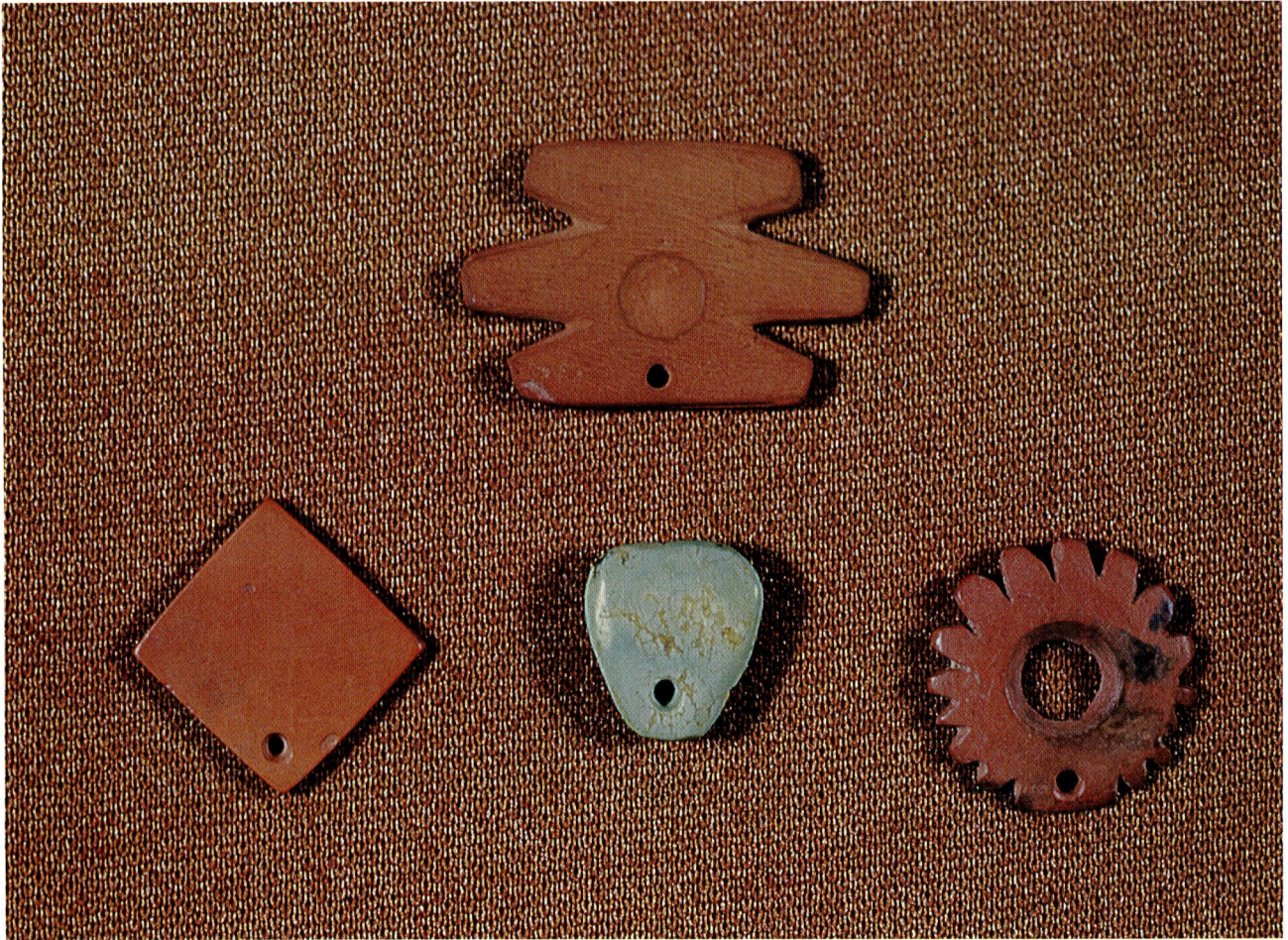

Pueblo III pendants

Clothing and Adornment

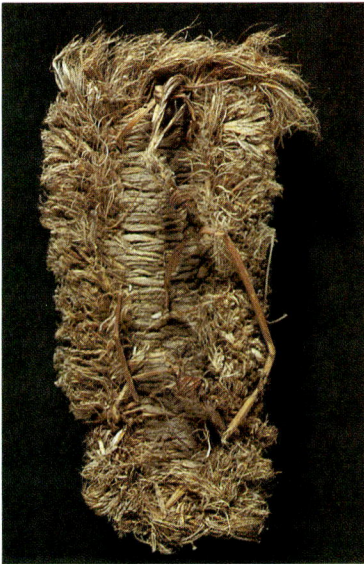

Basketmaker II sandals were of two main kinds: 4-warp wickerwork (top) and multiple-warp cord. The simpler wickerwork sandals may have been for everyday wear—or perhaps men and women used different styles.

The Anasazi country is a land of rocky cliffs, hot sands, and plants with stickers. This means that some sort of protection for the feet is a must. The Anasazi and most other southwesterners, with the exception of the moccasin-wearing Fremont people, usually used sandals. BMII people made sandals of two different styles. One type was made rather quickly out of partially mashed yucca leaves. These sandals were of wickerwork, made with four warps of a few leaves each—with additional leaves woven back and forth across them. The heels were knotted together, but the warps were left sticking out at the square toe to form a fringe. The ends of the leaves were left sticking out on the bottom of the sandal to form a padded sole. Occasionally, the leaves also were left on the sides—to form a fringe the entire way around. Sandals usually had a loop for the second toe, with additional leaves or strings used to tie them onto the feet.

A second type of BMII sandal was made of string. The string itself had to be prepared laboriously from yucca, apocynum, or other fibrous plants, scraped to leave nothing but fibers and then twisted into string. These sandals have from 15 to 36 cord warps running the length of the sandals. Additional string was woven in a tight tapestry weave over the warps. The toes were finished with a few rows of twining to hold them together, and, again, the warps were left sticking out to make a square, fringed toe. Occasionally, fringed buckskin was added at the toe. Since a pair of these sandals might use hundreds of feet of string (one pair used 1200 feet for the ties alone), one might suspect that their use was confined to special occasions—with the wickerwork sandals being the everyday wear. However, both types are found in about equal numbers, and both usually in worn out condition—leading one to suspect that either some people were not into fancy sandals or

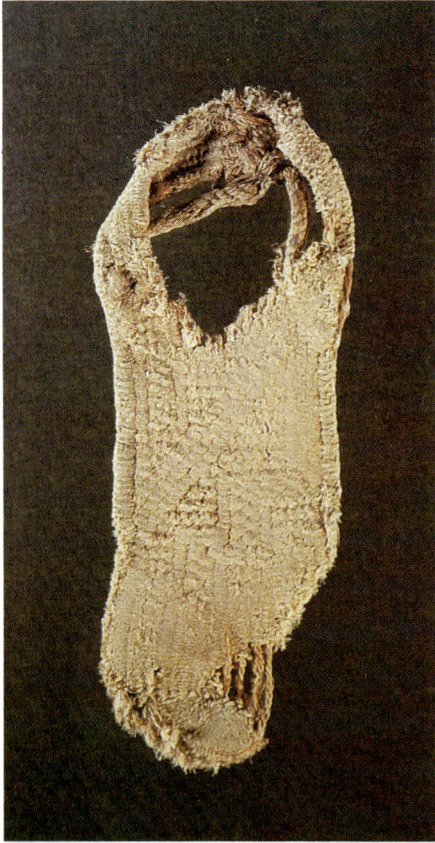

Basketmaker III people made their cord sandals even fancier, with elaborate raised designs on the soles.

Cord sandals gradually went out of style, and by Pueblo III, most Anasazi wore plaited (right) and twilled (left) sandals.

Mexican macaws were traded as far north as Chaco Canyon, where the Anasazi sometimes carved replicas of these exotic birds.

that women wore one kind and men the other. If so, it is most likely that men wore the more elaborate ones since they seem to have been more concerned with their appearance than the women.

In late BMII, and well into BMIII, the cord sandals became very elaborate, with raised designs on the soles and colored designs woven in or painted on. BMIII sandals typically were zoned, with the heel portion made of one weave, the central portion highly decorated, and the toe made of another kind of weave. The toes most often are concave, without a fringe. After BMIII, sandal making declined in quality, and new types, such as plaited sandals, came into use.

Clothing reflected the exigencies of climate. For cold weather, hide cloaks or shirtlike garments were worn most often, and fur blankets were common. The blankets, several feet square, were made by wrapping strips of rabbit skin around heavy strings and then weaving these furry strings together with rows of twining to form a blanket. Fur blankets and other garments probably were worn only in the coldest months, and a typical Basketmaker usually wore little more than sandals and a smile in the summer. Nothing identifiable as a hat has yet been found.

Babies had their own special fur blankets, with a notch at the bottom so the blanket wouldn't get soiled. Babies were tied snugly to oval cradles made of small sticks, and the newborn were provided with soft umbilical pads. BMII women occasionally wore menstrual pads or "aprons" of long strips of juniper bark brought between the legs and looped over a waist string in front and back. By BMIII, these aprons were finely woven of string with elaborate designs and may have held a wad of juniper bark only during the crucial part of the month.

Anasazi clothing remained sparse in ensuing centuries, and a great deal of it was worn as much for decoration as it was for protection. BMIII and later people continued to make fur blankets but also started making feather blankets. These were created in about the same way but had split turkey feathers wound around the strings instead of fur strips.

Some of the finest examples of early Anasazi weaving were found in Obelisk Cave, a BMIII site in northeastern Arizona. Here, archaeologists found six sashes made entirely of dog hair. The sashes, now at Mesa Verde Museum, were found tied together in a bundle and are as beautiful and soft today as they were at the time they were made about 1500 years ago. These six sashes, of varying combinations of brown and white dog fur, used a total of over a mile of finely spun dog hair string, which had been braided carefully into these fine sashes.

By PIII times, loom weaving was common, and cotton ponchos, as well as blankets, are found. The Anasazi continued to be fine weavers into historic times.

Although clothing usually was minimal, the Anasazi, like other people, liked to decorate their bodies. The men, particularly, seem to have been interested in their looks, for they wore their hair long—braided or tied in various ways. BMII women probably wore their hair irregularly cropped short because they continually were making string from it. By Pueblo times, however, the women, or at least the younger set, also were wearing their hair in elaborate hairdos. From Pueblo I on, the Anasazi were not content with simply changing their hair but went one step further and changed the shape of their heads. This was done by strapping the babies down to a hard cradleboard for practically all of the first months of life. As the head grew, it grew sideways, and the back of the head ended up flat. The Anasazi must have felt that this was pleasing in appearance. It also helped to set the Anasazi apart visually from other groups.

Men, women, and children all wore jewelry—particularly necklaces, pendants, bracelets, and

Basketmaker II turkey feather bundles, possibly worn as earbobs (above). Turquoise was a popular trade item in the prehistoric Southwest (below).

Pueblo III hair ornaments

rings. Even in BMII times, large quantities of olivella and abalone shell beads were being imported from the California coast. BMII people also made beads from bones, seeds, and variously colored stones. By Pueblo III, shells from both the California coast and the Gulf of California were popular trade items. Beads and pendants were carved from jet, bone, turquoise, argillite, and other minerals; mosaic work was practiced, and copper bells from Mexico found their way to Chaco Canyon. Not all PIII jewelry was obtained by trade. In some areas, PIII people systematically looted the graves of their BMII predecessors, removing the jewelry and scattering the bones about.

The Anasazi evidently always liked feathers, from which their hair ornaments often were made. Brightly colored feathers were most prized, so Mesoamerican traders had no trouble peddling feathers, and even live macaws, in this region. At Pueblo Bonito, the macaws were kept in some of the deepest and darkest rooms and rarely saw the light of day. It seems likely that the Anasazi exported large quantities of turquoise in exchange for the jewelry and other trade items.

Most people probably wore some jewelry all the time, but for special occasions, such as important ceremonies, the fancy blankets, elaborate hairdresses, and jewelry-bedecked bodies must have been quite impressive.

Anasazi strings of various materials, twists, and sizes

Basketry and Textiles

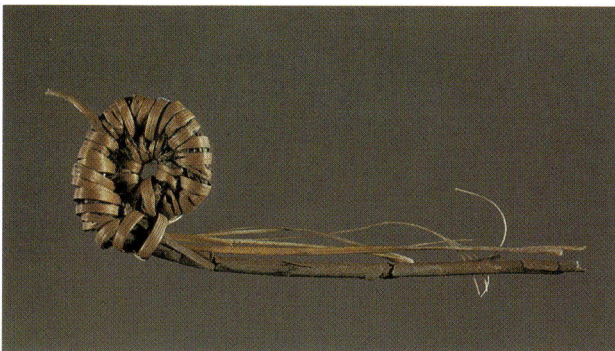

Coiled baskets were started at the center, spiraling outward by sewing the continuous foundation to the previous coil (above). Bone awls were a necessary part of every basketmaker's tool kit (below).

Baskets were made at least as early as 10,000 years ago in western North America, so that, by the time of BMII, many different shapes, styles, and techniques had been developed. The earliest Anasazi aptly are named Basketmaker II because their baskets were of extremely high quality. The baskets ranged in size from a few inches to several feet in diameter and often were decorated with geometric designs in black. Some were so tightly woven that they still are waterproof.

Making a basket is no simple task. The construction of even a small basket often involved more than 100 hours of labor. First, the materials (willow, squawbush, or other supple twigs) must be gathered and then split and split again, to get a thin, pliable sewing splint a foot or more long. These splints could be kept indefinitely if they were soaked before use to make them pliable.

Most BMII baskets were made by coiling, a technique that uses a foundation of twigs or split twigs wrapped with the sewing splints. Each splint binds the successive coil to the previous one. One of the more common shapes is a shallow tray, 1 to 2 feet in diameter, that was used to hold dried or ground foods. Judging from the charred interiors of some of these trays, they occasionally were used for parching, a way of cooking seeds by means of adding hot coals and shaking the basket until the seeds are cooked. Basketry bowls a foot or so in diameter were used frequently for stone boiling. Hot stones were dropped into the liquid or mush to cook the food. Small "trinket baskets" with a narrow opening seem to have been used for personal effects. Large, conical carrying baskets, thirty or more inches in diameter, were used for gathering and carrying plant foods. The basket would be balanced on the back, with a wide opening to make it easy for the person gathering seeds to throw them over her shoulder into the basket as she moved along. The basket, in order to leave the hands free, was carried by means of a tumpline attached to the basket and then passed across the forehead. Most BMII tumplines were of an undecorated, warp-faced fabric that sometimes was made of human hair string.

The Anasazi made a wide variety of string, from tiny, single-ply threads to heavy rope, out of yucca and other plant fibers, dog hair, human hair, and cotton. They used it in all the ways one can use string—for tying bundles of things, tying things together, attaching sandals to their feet, and for weaving. Regional differences among the Anasazi are apparent as early as Basketmaker II. In the west, BMII people scraped the yucca leaves or apocynum with implements made out of split mountain sheep horn. In the east, where deer were

more plentiful, they would split deer metapodials for the purpose. In the west, the two strands of yarn comprising a typical string were twisted in the opposite direction from that in the east. One of the more typical BMII items was a small, flexible bag made out of apocynum fiber. These twined bags were six to eight inches across and usually had geometric designs woven in or painted on. They seemed to have served largely as containers for personal items.

Basketmaker III basketry is similar to that of BMII in many respects, with one of the most significant changes being the addition of twilled baskets. These were made by interweaving yucca leaves in an over two, under two, or over three, under three pattern into a flat mat and then attach-

Baskets were complemented by flexible bags woven of string.

32

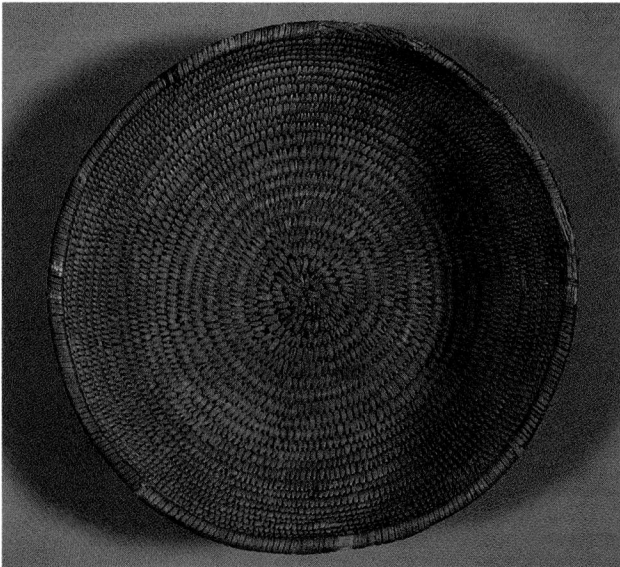
Coiled basket from Long House made with split willow. Some Anasazi baskets were so tightly woven they would hold water, and all show a high degree of skill.

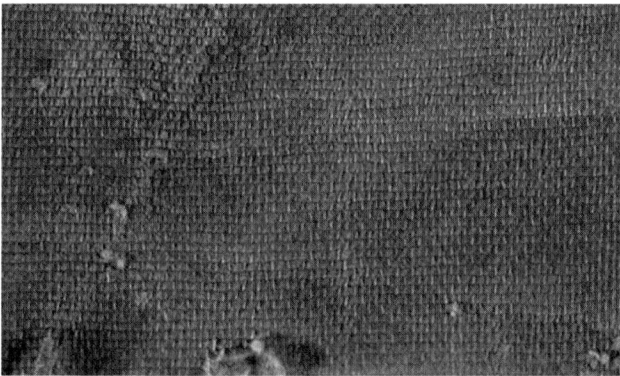
The Anasazi wove many fabrics on the loom, sometimes with more than 50 threads per inch.

ing this to a circular, wooden ring—creating a shallow bowl. These bowls may have been used as sifters but probably were more frequently used as general purpose containers. Other baskets were more elaborately decorated in BMIII than in BMII. Twined bags continued through BMIII, but they frequently were undecorated. Tumplines become very fancy, often made of fine tapestry weave and decorated with woven or painted designs.

We know rather little of Pueblo I and II basketry and textiles because PI and PII people did not live frequently in caves, where such things would be preserved. In late PIII, when the Anasazi moved back into caves for defensive reasons, we can see that they still were making fine baskets, as well as other kinds of textiles. One interesting PIII basket shape is the bifurcated basket. These sometimes are referred to by archaeologists as burden baskets, but the relatively small size of many of them, and the distinctive shape, suggests a special use. They probably were not used for carrying babies since cradleboards of several varieties continued. It seems more likely that they were used as containers for special ceremonial paraphernalia.

There is a fairly common impression that once the Anasazi started making pottery, basketmaking declined both in quantity and quality. At least up through PIII, however, the Anasazi were making a profusion of very fine baskets, and some of the most complicated weaves and intricate shapes come from PIII.

From what little we know of PIV basketry, it seems to have become somewhat less finely made. Baskets served many purposes that pottery could not, and it was not until the twentieth century, with the introduction of factory-made containers, that basketmaking declined rapidly. Today, baskets are made in only a few pueblos, mainly for the tourist and collector. The amount of time and effort needed to produce a fine basket is not appreciated by most casual tourists, so prices and demand may not be high enough to keep the craft alive for much longer.

The Anasazi wove numerous additional items out of string and other flexible materials—mats for the floor and as door coverings, carrying nets and hunting nets, snares, straps, blankets, and ponchos. Some of the PIII or PIV loom-woven fabrics are of very intricate weaves and elaborate decoration. The advent of cheap (and not so cheap) yard goods has meant that weaving, too, is almost a lost art among the Pueblos. The tradition is being carried on by the Navajo, however, who learned it from the Pueblos more than a century ago. In addition, some Hopi men have special rooms for weaving, a practice that started in PIII.

Awatovi Polycrome. One of the finest Pueblo IV pots excavated to date.

Pottery

McElmo Black-on-white pitcher, Mesa Verde area, Pueblo III (top) and Basketmaker III Lino Black-on-gray (bottom)

One of the attractions of the Southwest to early explorers, archaeologists, and relic collectors was the abundance, quality, and variety of Anasazi pottery. The very term "pothunter" conjures up visions of someone ruthlessly rooting out burials, scattering bones, breaking through house walls, and taking home the whole pots they managed to extract from the earth to impress their friends or to sell to others who want to own a "conversation piece." Most archaeologists and government officials concerned with preserving the past think that a mild form of punishment for pothunters would be to lock them into a rat-infested cell and throw the key away. However, early archaeologists were little better. Much of the emphasis before the turn of the century was on obtaining specimens for museum collections, with scant attention paid to the provenience, associations, and stratigraphic position of the artifacts that were dug up. Since the amount of information that can be derived from artifacts is directly proportional to the care with which they are excavated and recorded, archaeologists understandably have little patience with pothunters or collectors who are intellectually a century behind the times.

Pottery is very useful for the study of prehistoric culture change. As anyone who has ever washed dishes knows, pottery breaks rather easily and, therefore, must be replaced constantly. With replacement, designs and shapes change as well, and the distribution in time and space of the various styles can be determined quite closely. Studying pottery involves more than just an analysis of shape and design. Physical and chemical tests are conducted on pigments; microscopic and petrographic analyses of the bodies of the pots are done, and new techniques such as thermoluminescence, X-ray diffraction, and neutron activation analysis are useful in determining the physical attributes of the pot, determining where it was made, and for dating.

Fortunately, broken pottery does not disintegrate, and most techniques of analysis can be done as well on potsherds as on whole pots. The high

35

The earliest Anasazi pottery, typified by this Lino Gray jar, was usually plain with simple shapes.

Kana-a Gray. Pueblo I cooking pottery with un-smoothed neck coils

Late Basketmaker III San Marcial Black-on-gray

Pueblo I designs are formed of thin parallel lines and solid elements. Symmetrical bowls and jars are in the majority, but duck-shaped vessels are not uncommon.

breakage rate of pottery means that large numbers of sherds are recovered during the course of an excavation. Ofttimes, months or years then are spent in the study of these sherds.

By the 1930s, southwestern archaeologists had become increasingly concerned with classifying the pottery they found and were able to distinguish many variations from one time and area to another. These differences became formalized as "types," with names such as Wiyo Black-on-white, Glaze III, Heshotauthla Polychrome, Moenkopi Corrugated, and Tusayan Black-on-red. These types are useful because archaeologists have a common understanding of what each type looks like and where it is found, so discussions, compari-

sons, and determination of trade activities are facilitated. Since the number of types continues to grow, it is doubtful that many archaeologists today know more than a portion of the hundreds of types that have been defined. For this reason, the beginning student often is overwhelmed.

Today, pottery studies usually are not limited to classifying the sherds into types. Cross-type studies by archaeologists of materials, form, finishes, layout, design elements, and other characteristics are proving to be useful. Even within a single type, one can see variation—most of it attributable to individual craftsmanship and artistry. It would be easy, indeed, to spend a lifetime studying Anasazi pottery.

Sosi B/W jar, Kayenta area PII (above).
Pitchers and tall mugs are common in
the Mesa Verde and Chaco areas during
Pueblo II (below).

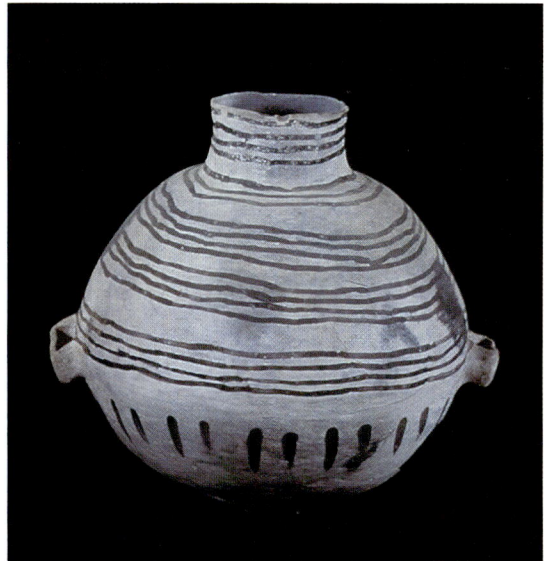

Mesa Verde water jars typically are globular with
strap handles below the shoulder.

The manufacture of pottery is more complex than chipping stone, building a house, or even making a basket, for several distinct steps are necessary. The last step, the firing, is the most important. Here, physical and chemical changes occur that convert the clay into a substance that will hold its shape permanently. The stresses that occur during firing are considerable, and all previous steps are performed with the firing in mind. Throughout Anasazi history, firing was done in an open fire. The Kayenta potters seemed to prefer either a nearby open spot or a sheltered depression, such as an abandoned pithouse. The PIII Mesa Verde potters constructed slab-lined kilns about four feet wide, ten feet long, and a foot deep. Such a pit not only protected the fire from the wind, but also provided more heat through radiation and reflection from the slabs.

Although clay is one of the more abundant substances on the earth's surface, not all clay is suitable for pottery. Some will crack or explode during firing, and some will not harden sufficiently except at temperatures beyond the range of a simple wood fire. Even so, the northern Southwest had many areas of suitable clays, deposited in layers in the distant geological past and later exposed on the sides of cliffs and canyons.

There is a distinct process in pottery making, and it has varied little over the centuries. First, the clay must be gathered, impurities picked out, and the clay ground up on a metate so that it will not be lumpy. Then, the dry, powdered clay is moistened to the proper consistency, and some kind of temper is added. Temper, which can be sand, crushed rock, or ground potsherds, is necessary to help keep the pot from cracking while drying and firing. The Anasazi built their pots by coiling. The coils then were smoothed by scraping. At this point, surfaces to be decorated often were slipped with a thin layer of fine clay, which then was polished and painted. After drying, the pots were fired, apparently by covering them with the wood and setting it on fire, though coal sometimes was used by the PIV people in the Hopi area. Anthropologists assume from analogy with modern Pueblos that pottery was made by women. Men may have helped with the gathering of clay and the painting. It is doubtful that all women were equally proficient. In fact, some women may not have made pottery at all. It is entirely possible that women became more specialized over the centuries—some concentrating on baskets, others on pottery, and still others on different items. Burials at a number of sites seem to support this possibility since some women were buried with potters' tools and others with different items.

Most Anasazi pots were made with round, rather than flat, bottoms. Without tables, round bases are no drawback since a round-bottomed cooking pot can be supported on a few rocks while heating up the stew. Round bottoms also are less likely to crack while drying and firing than are flat ones. Decoration varied with use. Jars, of course, have their decoration on the outside, whereas bowls are decorated on the inside. Again, with no furniture or cupboards, the bowls would be stored on the floor, with the inside as the visible portion.

Fifty years ago, some archaeologists thought that the Anasazi invented pottery without any outside influence from neighboring groups. We do know that BMII people sometimes lined baskets with mud to keep them from burning while parching seeds; and if one of these mud linings accidentally ended up in a fire, they would have had something similar to pottery. However, the earliest BMIII pottery does not resemble these mud-lined baskets, and recent evidence shows that the Mogollon and other people to the south of

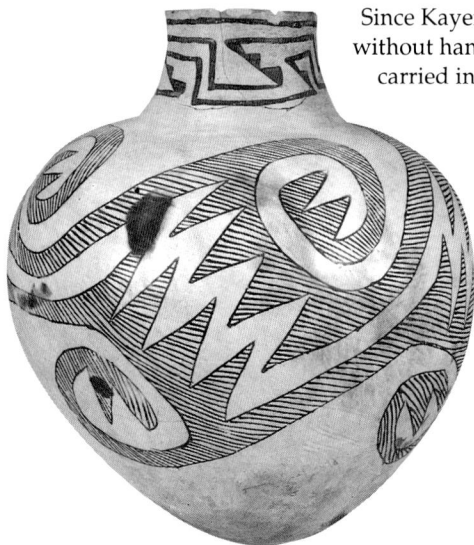

Since Kayenta water jars usually are without handles, they probably were carried in a loose net or rope sling. The hatched style of Dogoszhi Black-on-white is found rarely on Black-on-white bowls.

Late Pueblo I designs (above) were formed of wider lines, culminating in the bold designs of Pueblo II, such as the Black Mesa black-on-white bowl (left).

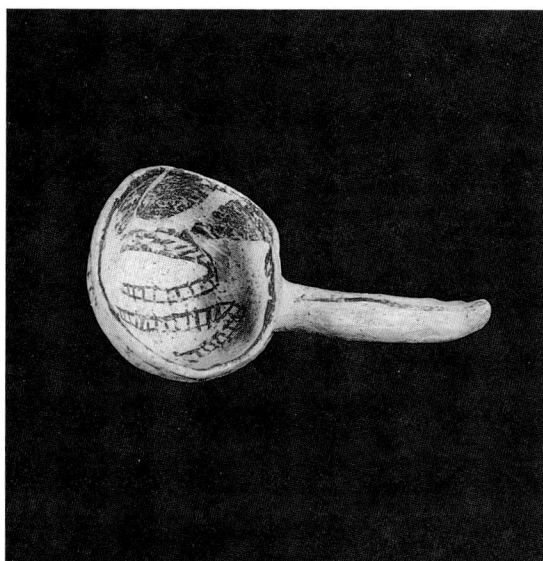

Dippers are common, whereas vessels of asymmetrical shapes occur only infrequently.

the Anasazi were making pottery before the Anasazi. It is more likely, therefore, that the idea of potterymaking diffused northward, ultimately from a Mesoamerican source.

Once the Anasazi learned to make pottery, they did not slavishly copy their Mogollon neighbors. Part of the distinctiveness of their work is the result of using different clays, but there are differences also in shapes and designs.

Early BMIII pottery was plain gray ware. Usually, it was only scraped; occasionally, however, we find a few polished pieces. Most shapes were simple, hemispherical bowls; wide-mouthed cooking jars; and large, narrow-mouthed jars. Since they were not bound by previous tradition, the BMIII people also experimented with other shapes—pots in the shapes of pumpkins and gourds, pots shaped like a hollow doughnut with a spout, duck-shaped vessels, and more. It is tempting to think that these strange shapes were ceremonial pieces, but they may reflect experimentation.

Soon, BMIII women began painting some of their bowls with simple designs. These designs are thought to be adaptations of basket designs, with simple lines and dots, but we have no way of telling what the design represents. The painted bowls generally were light gray in color to contrast with the black paint, whereas other pots were gray, brown, or almost black. Among the western Anasazi, as in the Kayenta area, the paint was organic, made from plant juices that carbonize during firing. To the east, paints were mineral, usually iron. These paints turn black in the reducing atmosphere the BMIII people obtained in their firing process. Sometimes, the pots were oxidized,

which caused the iron paint to turn red. The designs on some BMIII pottery from southwestern Colorado were painted with lead ore, which turned to a dark, greenish glaze when fired. Western Anasazi pottery also differed from the eastern in that the tempering material usually was sand, while in the east, crushed rocks were used more commonly.

Apparently, many BMIII people were not satisfied with the gray appearance of their pottery, for often, especially for the larger jars, they covered the pot after firing with a coat of red ocher. Perhaps they envied the brownish-red pottery made by the Mogollon.

By PI times, pottery was a well-established part of Anasazi life. Some of the eccentric BMIII shapes, particularly duck pots, continued, but painted wares now were more common. In this period, jars as well as bowls were painted, though a great deal of pottery still was undecorated (it makes little sense to decorate a cooking pot). The plain, gray pottery looks similar to that of BMIII, except that the last few coils on the neck of a jar usually were not smoothed on the exterior, resulting in a neck-banded effect.

The PI black-on-white pottery was made with a clay that fired to a light gray to white color or was slipped with white clay. Common design elements were thin, straight lines that often did not meet at the corners, solid triangular elements, and pendant dots or ticking along lines.

It is possible that we again see Mogollon influence, for about this time, the Anasazi in southeastern Utah made pottery that fired orange and was decorated with with simple, broad-line, red designs. A little black-on-red also has been found.

Medicine Black-on-red and Tusayan Black-on-red. Kayenta potters produced large numbers of redware vessels. Bowls are common, as are neckless jars usually known as seed jars.

Kiet Siel polychrome and Tusayan polychrome. During Pueblo III, the Kayenta potters were experimenting with various combinations of orange, red, black, and white.

These rapidly became popular trade items in PI but lost favor during PII and PIII, as the Kayentas began making better red ware.

Pueblo II cooking and storage pottery no longer was plain gray ware. During this period, the pieces were corrugated on the exterior. These corrugations were made by attaching each thin coil of clay to the one below with separate pinches of the fingers without smoothing them over. The interiors, of course, were smoothed. PII corrugated pottery usually was very well done, with bold, even corrugations, and the potter's fingerprints often still show in each pinch mark. There have been some attempts to use these fingerprints as a means of determining which pots were made by the same potter (and to use this information to trace trade relationships), but, so far, these at-

tempts have not been fruitful. Corrugated pottery works well for cooking purposes because more surface area is exposed to the fire. It is possible, however, that corrugated ware was made for its aesthetic effect.

PII black-on-white pottery typically is well polished, with bold and striking designs. Thick, solid lines; triangles; pendant dots; hatching; and other strong, geometric forms are common.

In the northern part of the Kayenta area, where suitable clays are found, PII women began making quite a bit of black-on-red pottery. Some designs on this black-on-red pottery developed into the striking polychrome pottery of the Kayenta area. Various combinations of black, red, and, sometimes, white paints on a red or orange background formed designs that differed from those of the

40

black-on-whites. These polychromes, made in the northern Kayenta region, were traded for black-on-white ceramics made in the central Kayenta area. They also were traded well outside the Kayenta region. Anasazi potters in the upper Little Colorado area also started making polychrome pottery in PIII, some of which also was traded widely.

During PIII, central Kayenta women also excelled in black-on-white pottery. Designs, in many cases, became negative—that is, so much black paint was used that the white background shows through as the design. Design layout also tended to be more complex, often with interlocking rectangular panels and circular scrolls that are remi-niscent of Hohokam pottery of the 1100s. Black-on-white pottery at Mesa Verde and the Rio Grande during PIII also was made nicely, but it had different, usually banded, layouts and simpler geometric elements. The largest sites in Chaco Canyon were built before the late PIII styles had been developed; therefore, the pottery associated with them looks more like typical PII pottery, with hatched designs being characteristic.

Not only did designs vary from one region to the next, but shapes also were somewhat different. For instance, Kayenta bowls often had a single handle near the rim, probably for hanging when the bowl was not in use. Mesa Verde potters made

Late Pueblo III Kayenta Black-on-white jar

Tusayan Black-on-white bowl, Pueblo III, Kayenta area

Pitchers with hatched designs were typical of the Chaco area during Pueblo III.

a lot of mugs, and special cylindrical jars have been found at Chaco. Other forms also differ from one region to the next, but less markedly.

Corrugated pottery continued into this period. It declined somewhat in quality, however, especially in the Kayenta area. By the end of PIII, most of the utility pottery in the region was just roughly finished, rather than deliberately corrugated.

The tempering traditions eastablished in BMIII times continued into PIII and beyond, with the western (Kayenta) Anasazi usually tempering their black-on-white pottery with sand, or even fine volcanic ash, whereas those in the east used

crushed rocks or crushed potsherds. The cooking pottery had temper of a larger fragment size, a thermodynamic necessity to keep the vessel from cracking when placed over a fire. Kayenta black-on-reds and polychromes, made of a different clay than the black-on-whites, needed sherd temper rather than sand. The Kayenta whitewares and red wares were made in different localities and used extensively as trade ware. We have found examples of poor quality red pottery being used for cooking. The Kayenta Anasazi used organic paints on their black-and-white, whereas the people at Mesa Verde preferred mineral paints for

42

South of the Chaco, it was common to decorate with opposite solid and hatched design elements. Canteens (right) would have been very useful in the arid Southwest.

Pueblo III Mesa Verde bowls usually have a banded design layout and ticks of paint along the square rim (above and right).

Mugs were a common form in Pueblo III during the Mesa Verde area.

Corrugated pottery continued to be carefully made in the Mesa Verde and Chaco areas (right) during Pueblo III, but became sloppy in the Kayenta area (left).

Many Pueblo IV Jeddito Black-on-yellow bowls of the Hopi area have designs that appear to be southern in origin.

45

Wiyo Black-on-white. Along the Rio Grande in New Mexico, many Pueblo III designs are similar to those of the Mesa Verde region.

Potsuwi Incised Jar, Pueblo IV, Rio Grande

Biscuit A (above) and Biscuit B (right) Pueblo IV bowls of the Rio Grande

the black on their white pots. Differences in materials can be traced to regional differences in the distribution of raw materials, and regional differences in design become more apparent through time.

By PII and PIII, Anasazi pottery traditions were moving south, and black-on-white and polychrome pottery was being made by groups that formerly had been making pots in the Mogollon fashion. Some people, like those in the Verde Valley, apparently never made their own black-on-white pots. Instead, they imported large numbers of them from the Kayenta and Little Colorado areas. It also is possible that some Kayenta Anasazi may have moved to the Verde Valley around this time.

Pueblo IV potters broke with tradition in many ways—new shapes, new color combinations, and

46

generally thicker vessel walls make PIV pottery quite distinctive. The reasons for the changes are obscure, but it is possible that there may have been an influx of Mesoamerican ideas during this period. The large population shifts and recombinations of people at the end of PIII meant that potters encountered techniques and clays that they were not familiar with. Black-on-white pottery generally died out and was replaced in the Little Colorado and Hopi areas by black-on-yellow and polychrome pottery on a yellow base. Jars were flattened vertically, and bowls tended to be more shallow, with incurving rims. Many designs show carryovers from Kayenta PIII pottery, but newer, birdlike designs may have been of southern derivation.

At the end of PIII in the upper Little Colorado region, pottery was being made with designs patterned after some of the Kayenta polychromes, though some of the paints were glazes. The use of glazes as paint spread to the Zuni area and then to the Rio Grande, where potters took it up enthusiastically but rather ineptly (glazes often ran during the firing, creating a messy design). With the brief exception of some of the BMIII pottery, mineral paints that actually melt at low temperatures had not been used previously by the Anasazi. Even in PIV, they were used only to create designs, not as

Jemez Black-on-gray bowls, Pueblo IV. The bowl with the terraced rim probably was used for special religious purposes.

Sankawi Black-on-cream vessels. The jar on the left has the Awanyu design, probably derived from the feathered serpent of Mesoamerica.

47

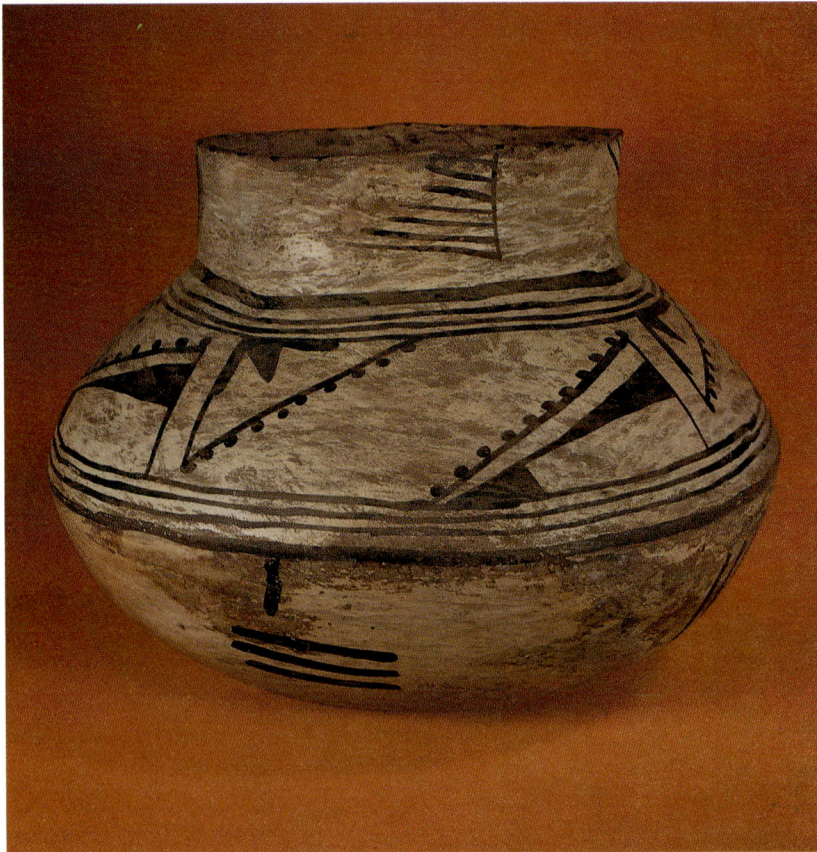

Pueblo IV Sankawi Black-on-cream jar

Kuau-a Glaze Polychrome vessel

Agua Fria Glaze-on-red and Espinosa Glaze Polychrome. The use of glaze paints became common in the Rio Grande during Pueblo IV.

Pueblo IV cooking pottery is usually unpretentious.

an overall glaze that would make the pot water-proof. Anasazi pots would hold water, and the smoothed and polished surfaces were easy to clean; but they were porous, and water could seep slowly through them. This was an advantage for water jars since the surface evaporation would help the water keep cool and sweet.

Pueblo IV cooking and storage pottery often is thought to be crude, compared to the fine PII and PIII corrugated wares. Frequently, it is rough, carelessly finished, and perhaps not as aesthetically pleasing, but it served its purpose well. Much of PIV pottery is considered to be inferior when compared to that of PIII. But some of it, particu-larly in the Hopi and Zuni areas, was very well made and superbly decorated.

With the coming of Europeans, Pueblo pottery did go into a decline. It was not just the advent of metal pots and pans that gradually replaced pottery but the European demands for labor and other disruptions that left less time for careful craft production. Pueblo women continued to make pottery, and with the coming of the railroad and tourists at the end of the nineteenth century, potters again found a market for their wares. In the last sixty years, quality has improved again, prices have soared, and the Anasazi pottery tradition looks far from dead.

49

Pueblo IV kivas had elaborate murals painted on the walls. Some of these murals are abstract designs, while others are scenes with people and supernatural beings. This one is a reconstruction of a mural from Awatovi.

Religious Life

The Anasazi lived in a land where the vagaries of nature could mean the difference between life and death. A prolonged drought would result not only in poor crops, but in poor hunting and poor gathering; flash floods could wipe out farms, and excessively cold winters could spell disaster.

The lack of food may not have resulted in actual starvation very often, but when people were weak, disease was able to make inroads, and the elderly and the young might not make it through the winter. Like other people at different times and places, the Anasazi tried to modify the forces that affected their well-being through influencing supernatural forces and beings. Since archaeologists cannot observe Anasazi religious beliefs and practices directly, our knowledge of their religion is based upon interpretations of artifacts and architecture that seem to have been used ceremo-

nially. Anthropologists also use analogies with current cultures, and southwestern archaeologists are fortunate that the Pueblo descendants of the Anasazi still retain a great deal of the Anasazi religious practices.

Basketmaker II religion seems to have been oriented toward individuals, especially during times of crisis, rather than toward organized and repeated community ceremonies. BMII people did not build any structures that appear to be ceremonial, nor do special ceremonial areas seem to have been set aside. Our main indications of BMII religion, therefore, come from burials, "medicine bundles," and "ceremonial objects." The "medicine bundles" do not seem to have been strictly ceremonial because they contain a heterogeneous collection of both practical and esoteric objects. They may be collections of an individual's

50

personal items, both secular and religious. To the BMII individual, the distinction may have been meaningless: the charm that ensured good hunting may have been considered just as necessary and practical as a good point on the spear. Any one "medicine bundle" may contain such items as spear points, sinew, a flaker for working stone, lumps of pigment, pretty stones, a pipe, little bags containing small objects, feathers tied together in various ways, and miscellaneous worked pieces of wood, stone, and bone. Although some of the items appear to be practical, they may have acquired powers through association with some person, place, or event, and perhaps all of these bundles could be considered entirely ceremonial.

BMII smoking pipes usually were short, made of clay or stone, and had a bone or wood mouthpiece stuck in the small end. In later times, similar pipes called "cloud-blowers" often were used in ceremonies to create images of clouds and help bring rain. It seems unlikely, however, that BMII people were yet that interested in weather control. Medicine men (shamans) over much of the Americas used the powerful wild tobacco as an aid in gaining the supernatural powers necessary to diagnose and cure illness, and Basketmakers probably were no exception.

BMII people like feathers. It is difficult to see how some feather bundles could have been worn, which means that they may have played some role in curing ceremonies. Small stones and miscellaneous objects may have been invested with particular powers or could represent evil things sucked out of an ill persons's body.

Bone whistles often are found in medicine bundles. Whistles are an integral part of the kit of many shamans, who used them in attracting or repelling the attentions of various spirits and to help the shaman acquire the proper state of mind.

Archaeologists often have a tendency to assign the label "ceremonial" to any object whose use is not readily apparent. There seems to be little doubt, however, that many BMII items were connected closely with religious ideas and practices. At this time, we can only guess and generalize about the subject, and specific beliefs are hard to define. We are reasonably certain that some objects—such as a human scalp, found with the hair still carefully done up—had ceremonial affinities. Perhaps the scalp was brought back by a raiding party so the proper observances could be held to prevent the spirit of the killed man from exacting vengeance. However, this particular scalp was found with the burial of an 18-year-old woman and her tiny baby and appears to have been suspended from the mother's neck by a pair of strings.

Another BMII item of presumed ceremonial use is a wooden "wand" about 6 inches long, with one end carved into a bird head, and an elaborate set of streamers tied to the center. These streamers are made of feathers, bird tails, small animal tails, and soft leather. Other items from various sites include stuffed bird heads, decorated bone tubes tied in pairs, and a host of other objects of unidentified purpose.

Basketmaker II people commonly buried their dead in caves, usually within the cists that had been dug into the cave floor. It is even possible that many of these cists had been constructed specifically to receive the body (or bodies—sometimes, several people were buried at the same time). On the other hand, perhaps the idea was to bury the dead as quickly as possible, and any abandoned cist would do. Perhaps a person used a particular cist for food storage during life, and it was considered appropriate to bury him or her in it after death.

Bodies were tightly flexed, with the knees drawn up to the chest. They were wrapped in a fur blanket or deerskin and accompanied by baskets, clothing, and personal items. The baskets often were "killed" by knocking out the bottom. Obviously, the survivors had some special feelings about the deceased—either honoring them or helping the spirit in the afterworld with the things that had been necessary in life.

Burials in later Anasazi times continued to have what can be called either offerings or personal possessions. During BMII and BMIII, most individuals were buried with about the same amount and types of things. By Pueblo III, however, there were some burials with next to nothing, while others had numerous offerings. This may reflect increasing status differences, the wealth of the deceased (or of a relative), the regard in which others held the deceased, or even the wishes of the deceased. In any event, the Anasazi clearly demonstrated some belief in an afterworld or life after death. Some burials indicate that women specialized in crafts, for tools and materials for basketmaking and pottery making have been found with different individuals.

Shamanistic practices also continued, as evidenced by medicine bundles and objects of no apparent utilitarian purpose. Sacred Datura, a hallucinogenic plant, is used today by some Pueblo shamans to help them reach the spirit world. Occasionally, it also is administered to patients. There are some canyons where the only Datura plants to be found are in Pueblo III cliff sites, an indication that the use of Datura may have started during that period.

Although burials can tell us a great deal about Anasazi society, they can raise as many questions as they answer. Sometimes, Anasazi individuals died away from home. If they were buried in a nearby village, we probably would not be able to tell, but some of the burials found in Anasazi sites are aberrant. We know, for example, that a Fremont individual was buried at Mesa Verde. Some of these individuals could have been traders or visitors. But might others have been there for different reasons? Another puzzle is the fact that the number of Anasazi burials found does not seem to fit the population estimates; perhaps some individuals were buried in special places.

Becoming increasingly important from BMIII on were ceremonies involving many individuals. The presence of kivas at practically all PIV sites indicates a kind of ceremonialism still found among modern Pueblo Indians. Religious observances also occurred in PII and PIII kivas, particularly during the warm months when surface rooms were used for habitation. PIV kivas may have been constructed by, and belonged to, a particular clan or society, yet other societies may have held primary responsibility for the ceremonies conducted therein. The ceremonies in PIII great kivas, involving large numbers of both participants and spectators, served in a similar fashion to unite the community.

Almost certainly, the ceremonies revolved around the seasonal cycle—renewal and rebirth at the winter solstice, fertility and growth in the spring, rain during the summer, and thanksgiving in the fall. If modern Pueblo practice can serve as an example, each ceremony involved months of planning and preparation. Secret parts of the ceremony probably lasted for days and culminated in a public peformance by men elaborately garbed to represent various supernatural beings. Some men probably served as part-time priests.

The time and effort that went into the construction of a great kiva is an indication of the importance of the ceremonies conducted in them. Even today, while sitting in a great kiva, such as Casa Rinconada at Chaco Canyon, it is not hard to visualize the fire in the center lighting the faces of the spectators dressed in their finery.

Kivas rarely were left with many artifacts in them since the sacred objects would be considered too valuable to leave behind. Some, however, are found with clay, pottery tools, and unfired pots on the floors—a clear indication that pottery manufacture also occurred within. Weaving, of course, was common in the kivas. Domestic items, such as grinding stones and ordinary pots, also are found. While it is clear that not all activity in the kivas was centered around religion, this appears to be its primary focus. The religious objects that we have found often are elaborately detailed and ornately decorated. Some PIII pottery seems to have been designed solely for religious uses. The Mesa Verde "kiva jars," the only southwestern pots with lids, could have been used for holding special ceremonial items. They may also have been used for sprouting beans. Kayenta "colanders," small jars with holes in the bottom, also may have been used

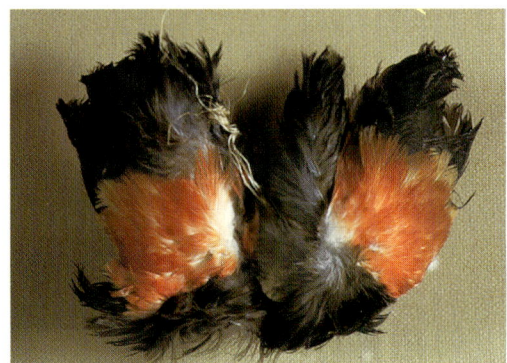

This "tablita" and the accompanying ear ornaments apparently were part of a ceremonial costume at Chaco Canyon (above). Anasazi pipes (top, right). These red-winged blackbird wing skins from a Basketmaker II cave may have served some ritual purpose—or perhaps they were being saved for decorations (bottom, right).

This small Walnut Black-on-white bird may have been used in religious ceremonies.

Pueblo III kiva jar from the Mesa Verde (right). It is the only type of southwestern pot with a fitted lid. The use of this vessel is not clear.

in this way. The sprouting of beans is important in some modern Pueblo ceremonies and may have been important in Anasazi ceremonies as well. The sprouts would have served as a good source of greens during the winter.

Other possible ceremonial pottery shapes include the duck pots, occasional pots shaped like parrots or other birds, lobed pots, jars with handles in the shape of an animal, the cylindrical jars from Chaco, and other shapes. Most of these have been found in situations that do not indicate clearly what they were used for.

Petroglyphs and pictographs pecked or painted onto cliff faces sometimes may have been little more than grafitti, but some of them may portray supernatural ideas. Basketmakers often portrayed large, trapezoidal-bodied human figures and fat-bodied mountain sheep. Pueblo III rock art consisted of geometric figures, hunting scenes, and, possibly, mythical beings. Some Pueblo III rock art is interpreted as clan symbols. Mountain sheep are common and may represent a successful hunt. Some mountain sheep groups have a hunter portrayed nearby. Many designs are geometric; spirals are common. We do not know what these symbols portrayed. Other designs may have represented snakes and mythical beings. Some, most obviously the sun dagger in Chaco Canyon, may help mark the movements of the sun. PIII people sometimes painted simple, geometric designs on their room walls, including those rooms called kivas. Pueblo IV kivas were elaborately decorated, many containing figures or groups of figures dressed much like historic kachina dancers. Some of these kivas were replastered and repainted many times. Kachina-like figures appear also on PIV pottery and on the sandstone cliffs.

From 100 to 1600 A.D., regional variations in religious practices are apparent, both archaeologically and historically, but the general pattern seems to have been one of increasing complexity, based in part on Mesoamerican ideas. Some architectural features that appeared during PIII seem to be derived from the more complex cultures far to the south. During PIV, for example, specific designs such as the feathered serpent, or Quetzalcoatl, are obvious signs of southern influence. Perhaps Mesoamerican traders bringing parrots and copper bells also brought religious ideas—or perhaps some Anasazi journeyed south and brought these ideas back. Compared to the empires of Mesoamerica, the Anasazi were a pretty marginal frontier group that would have been easily impressed by the grandeur of Mesoamerican religion and artifacts.

A common motif in rock art appears to be a person with a large back, playing a flute. This individual, known as kokopelli, often is thought of as a hunchback but more likely represents a trader with a pack full of goodies. Perhaps his flute playing was widely admired or served to announce his arrival.

Many Pueblo Indians were not impressed by Christianity, especially since the Spanish tried to force it upon them. Despite the intense acculturation pressures by Spanish and later Anglo missionaries, Pueblo religion did not disappear. Instead, it literally went underground. Ceremonies were, and in many cases still are, performed secretly in the kivas, with no outsiders allowed. The Pueblos have learned the hard way that although their ceremonies are for the good of all, they leave themselves open to persecution and ridicule if they allow everyone to take part in them—even as spectators. Religious tolerance was greater among the Anasazi than among Christians. Every pueblo had its own religious observances, and differences are apparent in the various regions.

Religious ideas spread widely and rapidly, and if Christianity had not had an exclusive nature, it seems likely that the Pueblos would have incorporated at least some tenets of Christianity into their beliefs.

The Anasazi of Chaco Canyon constructed roads leading off in many directions, using them for trade, travel, and transportation of building timbers. When they met the edge of canyons, the roads descended by means of stairways cut into the rock.

Conclusion

Even the casual visitor to the Anasazi country cannot fail to notice the contrast from pine-covered mountains to bare sand dunes, flat plains to deep canyons, sandstone cliffs to lava flows, and the bare desert floor to a cool spring. If the visitor moves out of the motel room, the difference between the hot days and cold nights becomes striking, and if she or he stays for a while, the summers seem too short and hot and the winters too long and cold.

Since the sun shines most of the time in the Southwest, the Anasazi were lucky if they got six inches of moisture during a year in some areas. There are many different wild plant foods and a fair number of edible animals on the Colorado Plateau, but it takes a lot of time and effort, gathering and walking, grinding and storing to be assured of enough food all year. It is no wonder that the Anasazi turned increasingly toward agriculture in order to eat. It was easier and more secure to plant corn and take care of the plants a bit than it was to hope that nature would provide.

Once a reliable food supply is provided by agriculture, fewer people die, and populations grow. A larger population means more people gathering the limited wild food and, therefore, more dependence on agriculture. This, in turn, leads to more population growth. In good years, the Anasazi could grow more corn and beans than they and their family could eat. This left time for making fine pottery, thinking up new dances, and talking about the origins of the universe and the creatures populating it.

We know from our own experience that not all years are good years, nor is it possible to practice agriculture everywhere. Much of the Four Corners area, where the Anasazi resided, is too high in elevation to grow crops. The growing season is long enough at the lower elevations, but the dry, hot summer in those areas is too much even for plants with their roots a foot or more in the ground.

One of the characteristics of southwestern climate is that it is rarely the same from one year to the next. Paleoclimatic studies, based on pollen analysis, tree-rings, arroyo cutting and deposition, and other factors, have shown that the Anasazi experienced the same sort of variations as have been evident in the last 50 to 100 years. Some years had wet winters, which is good for planting, but dry, windy summers, which makes it hard for the crops to mature. Other winters may have been dry and the summers wet, and almost any sort of combination can occur. Some decades seem to have been more favorable, whereas others were genuine droughts.

Longer periods also have witnessed fluctuations. There is increasing evidence that moisture patterns in the Southwest (and elsewhere) follow a cycle of about 550 years. Thus, the years A.D. 600 and 1150 were at the optimum for moisture, whereas 875 and 1425 were the driest portions of the cycle. The cycle is so long that no one person would notice any appreciable difference during his lifetime, but it is interesting to note that the times when the Anasazi seem to have been most vigorous, expanding in both population and ideas, were during the wettest portions of the cycle—BMII and BMIII in the 500s to 700s, and PII and PIII in the 1000s to 1200s.

These climatic optimums were followed by a great deal of movement and consolidation in a few favorable spots in PI and PIV. Climatically poor periods also saw social disruption from newcomers to the Anasazi area and the aggradation into larger villages, probably for defense.

The Anasazi did very well, considering the problems they faced. In cold, wet periods, they farmed the lower elevations, and in warm dry times, they moved their farms to higher elevations. Warm, wet years were bonanzas, and they were able to harvest enough to last an extra year or two. The cold and dry years literally were the killers, especially if several occurred in succession. Even within the past century, there have been times when Pueblos died of starvation and the diseases that were able to take hold when the people were not strong. As far back as BMII, mass burials took place. It is not pleasant to think of the shock and grief that must have been felt throughout the small community when a young mother and her infant, a strong elder cousin, and a grandmother all died within a few hours of each other.

One particularly tragic event occurred in northern New Mexico at the Salmon Ruin. One of the main kivas there had burned with a very intense fire. On top of the burned roof, and burned with it, were the bodies of about nineteen children. We probably never will know what happened, but perhaps an epidemic struck the town, causing the death of many children, and the blame was associated with that particular kiva.

It is a mistake to think that the Anasazi were concerned only with survival, however. Bone dice are found commonly at BMII sites. Eight to ten oval bones about an inch long and two or three circular ones comprised a set. The oval bones were incised on one side and coated with pitch or ochre, and the round bones have a small hole drilled partially into the center of one face. It must have been a complicated and exciting game, with 44 possible combinations in the lay of the dice alone, not even considering their arrangement.

Anasazi sites frequently yield miniature pots; some were made by experienced potters, while others appear to be the work of amateurs. It is possible that men made a few pieces for special ceremonial purposes, but it is pleasant to think that many were toys, made either by little girls or their mothers.

We have found small clay figurines made in BMII times. Most of these figures are female, and anthropologists often believe that they have some connection with fertility ceremonies. Since miniature carrying baskets made of clay also are found, and are of a size to correspond to the size of the figurines, it seems likely that they were ceremonial. Perhaps the figurines and baskets were used to ensure a plentiful harvest. It also is possible that they were toys—dolls used by little girls in a re-enactment of daily activities.

Any Anasazi village would have had infants crying, toddlers getting into things they should not, and older children hoping to grow up and become full-fledged members of the community. At about the time of puberty, they probably were initiated into the mysteries of religion and marriage. Only after the hard times of trying to provide for a family were passed would it be possible for them to turn to more leisurely pursuits, such as weaving, pottery making, keeping track of the movements of the sun and planets, and telling stories to the grandchildren.

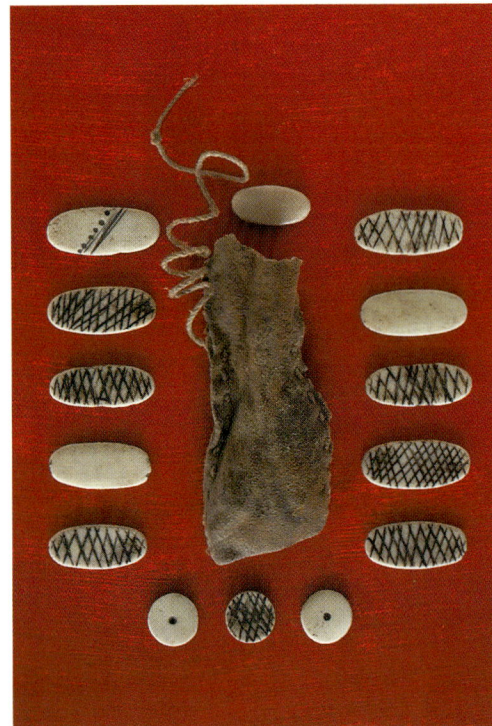

The Anasazi liked to gamble. This set of bone gaming pieces was found in the little leather bag. Basketmaker II, Sand Dune Cave

This miniature corrugated pot may have been a toy.

Summer and fall were the busy times and, if the harvest was good, the winter would be a time for crafts, intrigues, dances, and visiting. Men sometimes may have been gone for months, off learning new curing techniques from a famous shaman, trading turquoise for shell, raiding, or just seeing the world. Not all Anasazi were the same. Some women were specialists in certain crafts, and some men were noted as being especially good priests or shamans, hunters, farmers, traders, or warriors.

The women were more closely bound to the home, and the house and all its furnishings may have belonged to a woman. She and her sisters, aunts, and grandmother probably formed the stable family unit. If a man did not like living with his mother-in-law, he could go home to his own mother; or, more likely, if his wife's relatives did not like him, they would kick him out. Men brought rain with their ceremonies, dug irrigation ditches when the rain was scarce, hauled rocks for house walls, felled logs for roofs and fires, and provided meat for the pot. A deer would have been the basis of a feast for people living on corn and beans— and well worth the days of looking and stalking to get within arrow or spear range.

The many backbreaking hours of grinding corn would make a woman old before her time, and everyone's teeth eventually were ground flat from the sand that comes from using stone tools for grinding food. Anasazi teeth would be a dentist's nightmare: horrendous cavities, gum loss, and other problems were common. Older people suffered from arthritis and rheumatism, and the very young died of malnutrition and pneumonia. People fell and broke their arms and legs, crushed their fingers under rocks, were stuck with cactus thorns, and were bitten by gnats. Sometimes, there were small raids, feuds, and wars. Occasionally, the victors ate the bodies of the losers.

They laughed in the good times and cried in the bad, made beautiful things for their homes and bodies, counted the days until spring, remembered the past, and worried about the future.

They denuded large areas of their forest cover, littered the ground in front of their houses with trash, caused tons of topsoil to be eroded away and depleted of nutrients, and filled their lungs with soot from the fires. When things got too tough or used up in one spot, they moved to another location. Probably, they moved sometimes just because they became bored with the same place or wanted a different view. In short, the difference between the Anasazi of 500 or 1000 years ago and the present people of the Southwest is more one of degree than of kind.

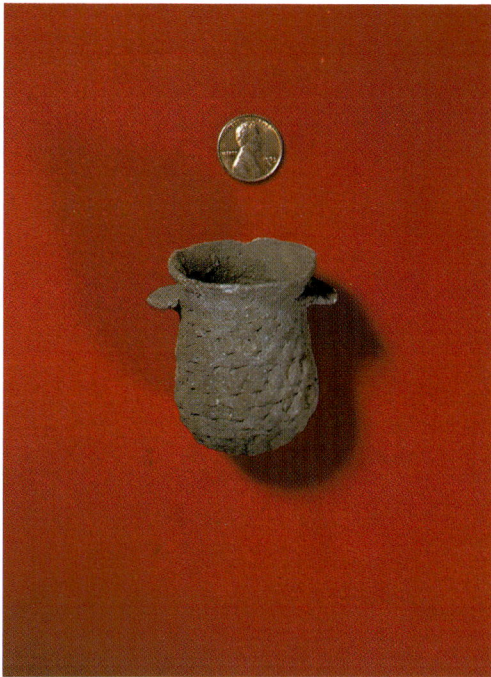

ADDITIONAL READING

Archaeologists are a wordy bunch, and the number of journal articles, technical works, site reports, and detailed summaries on the Anasazi is enough to fill many bookshelves. Listed here are those of more widespread interest, especially those that have been published recently. Many are in print, and all should be available at any university library. This is not intended as an exhaustive, or even representative, listing, but the interested reader will find more detailed bibliographies in these.

Ambler, J. Richard
  1985 Navajo National Monument: An Archaeological Assessment. Northern Arizona University Archaeological Series 1.

Bullard, William R., Jr.
  1962 The Cerro Colorado Site and Pithouse Architecture in the Southwestern United States prior to A.D. 900. *Papers of the Peabody Museum, Harvard University*, Vol. XLIV, No. 2

Cordell, Linda S.
  1984 *Prehistory of the Southwest.* Academic Press, Orlando, Florida.

Eddy, Frank W.
  1966 Prehistory in the Navajo Reservoir District, Northwestern New Mexico. *Museum of New Mexico Papers in Anthropology* No. 115, part II.

Fox, Nancy
  1985 Prehistory and History in the South west. *Papers of the Archaeological Society of New Mexico* No. 11, Santa Fe, New Mexico. (Also, nos. 1-10 in this series.)

Hayes, Alden C.
  1964 The Archaeological Survey of Wetherill Mesa, Mesa Verde National Park, Colorado. *National Park Service Archaeological Research Series* No. 7-A.

Jennings, Jesse D.
  1966 Glen Canyon: A Summary. *University of Utah Anthropological Papers*, No. 81.

Judd, Neil M.
  1954 The Material Culture of Pueblo Bonito. *Smithsonian Miscellaneous Collections*, Vol. 123

Lindsay, Alexander J., J. Richard Ambler, Mary Anne Stein, and Philip M. Hobler
  1968 Survey and Excavations North and East of Navajo Mountain, Utah 1959-1962. *Museum of Northern Arizona Bulletin* 45.

Martin, Paul S. and Fred Plog
  1973 *The Archaeology of Arizona.* Doubleday/Natural History Press, New York.

McGregor, John C.
  1965 *Southwestern Archaeology.* University of Illinois Press, Urbana, Illinois.

Morris, Earl H. and Robert Burgh
  1941 *Anasazi Basketry.* Carnegie Institution of Washington, Publication 533.

Oppelt, Norman T.
  1981 *Guide to Prehistoric Ruins of the Southwest.* Pruett Publishing Co., Boulder, Colorado.

Plog, Fred and Walter Wait
  1982 *The San Juan Tomorrow.* National Park Service, Santa Fe, New Mexico.

Shuler, Linda Lay
  1988 *She Who Remembers.* (A novel concerning a 13th century Anasazi woman.)

Smith, Jack E., ed.
  1983 Proceedings of the Anasazi Symposium, 1981. Mesa Verde Museum Association.

Smith, Watson
  1971 Painted Ceramics of the Western Mound at Awatovi. *Papers of the Peabody Museum, Harvard University*, Vol. 37.

Stuart, David E. and Rory P. Gauthier
  1981 *Prehistoric New Mexico: Background for Survey.* State of New Mexico Historic Preservation Bureau, Santa Fe, New Mexico.

Tanner, Clara Lee
  1976 *Prehistoric Southwestern Craft Arts.* University of Arizona Press, Tucson, Arizona.

Vivian, Gordon and Paul Reiter
  1960 The Great Kivas of Chaco Canyon and their Relationships. *Monographs of the School of American Research*, No. 22.

Wilcox, David R. and W. Bruce Masse, eds.
  1981 The Protohistoric Period in the North American Southwest, AD 1450-1700. *Arizona State University Anthropological Research Papers* No. 24, Tucson, Arizona.